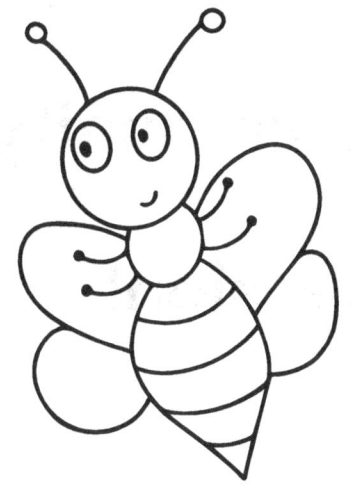

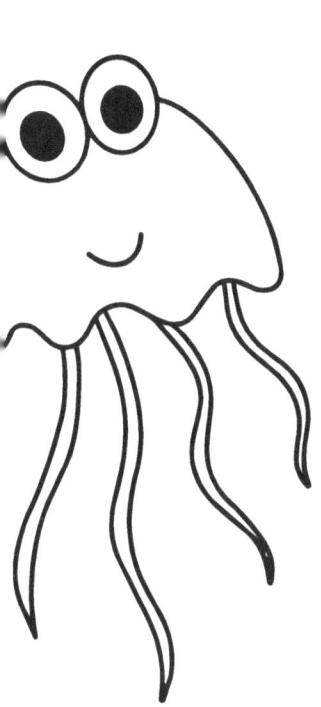

How to Draw

Cute Animals

for Kids

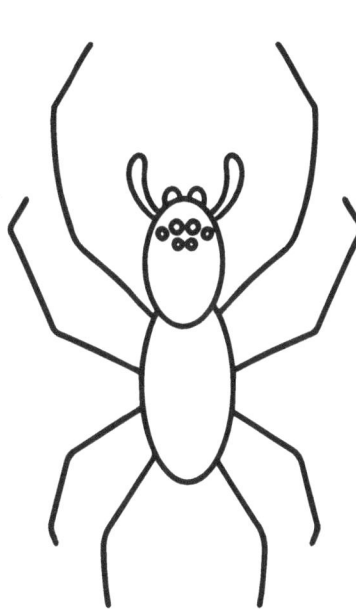

By
Inno Infinitas

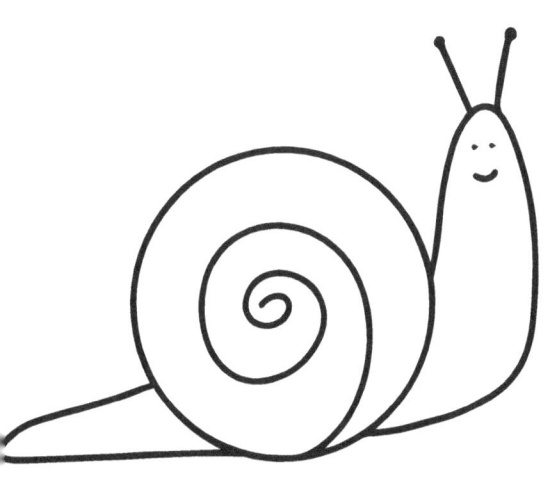
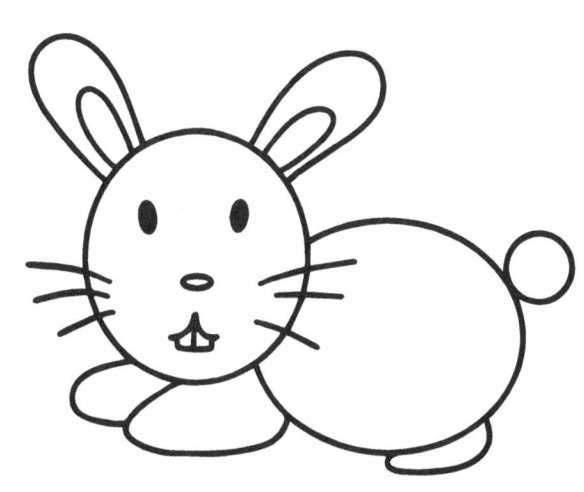

Share your artwork with community and
get your FREE digital version!

Please kindly share it with us in the community. Thank you so much.Visit our community here:

https://bit.ly/3BnaVgx

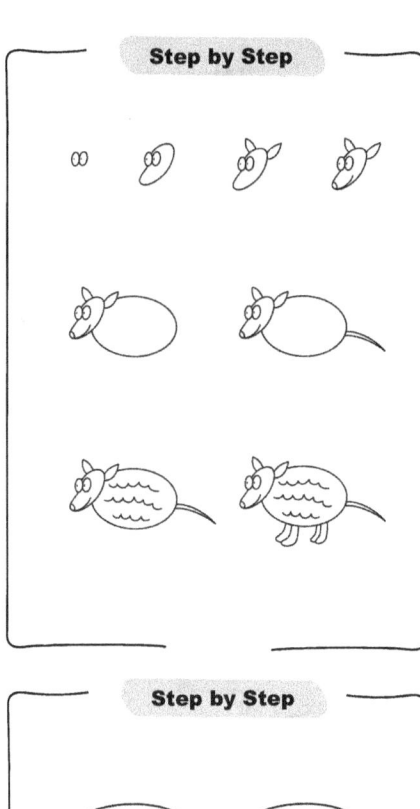

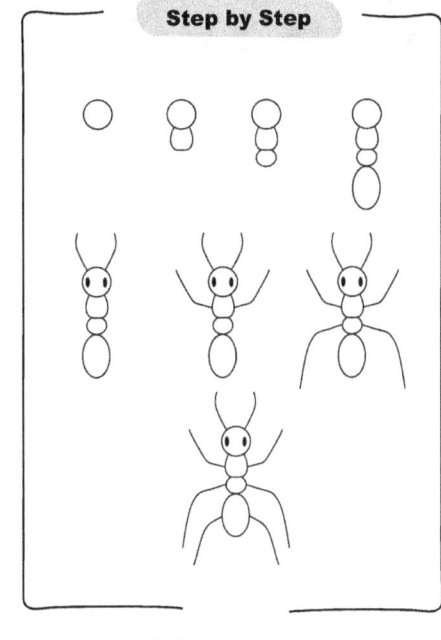

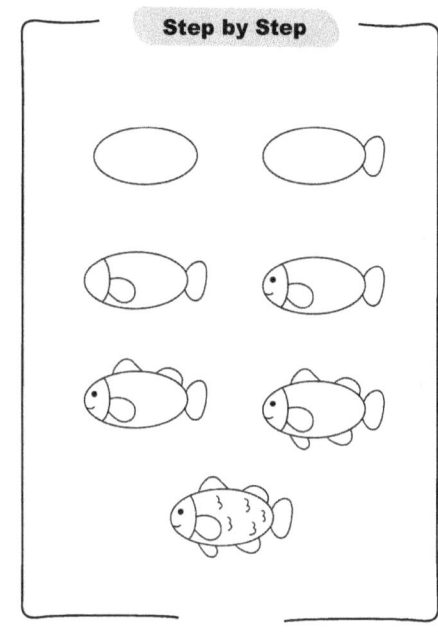

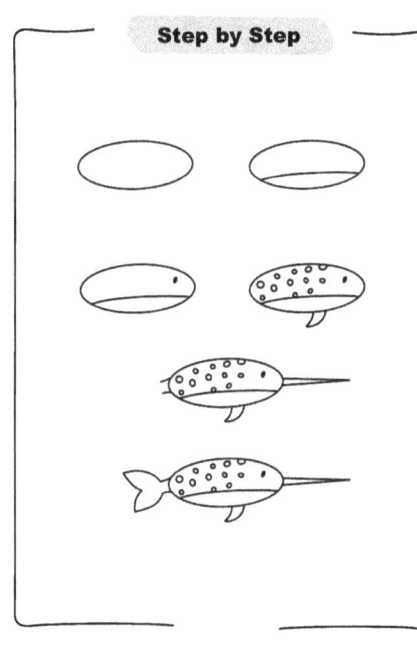

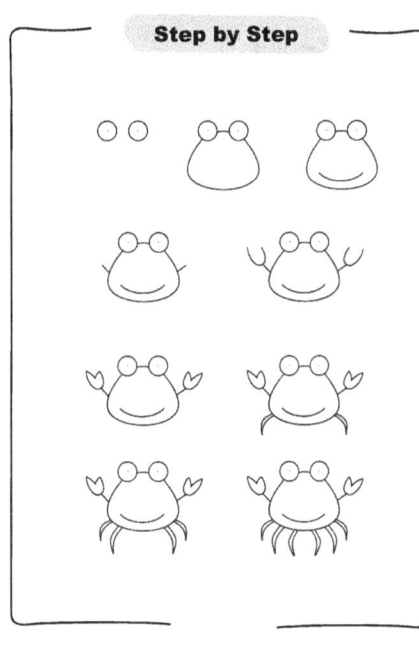

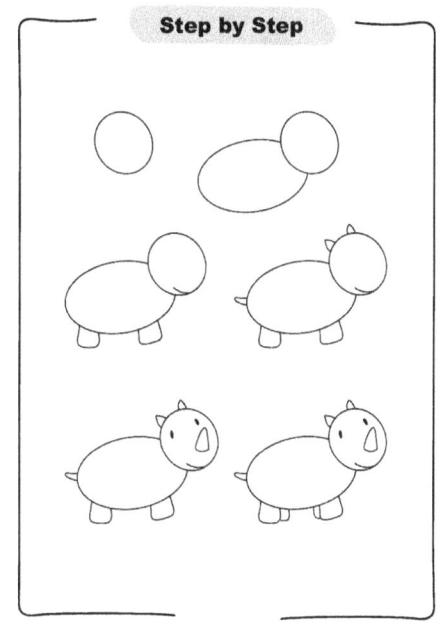

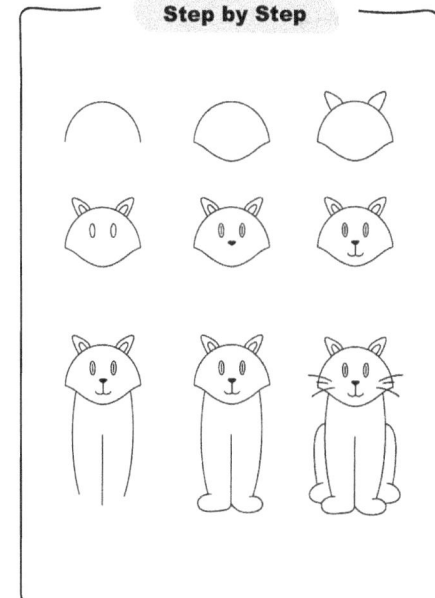

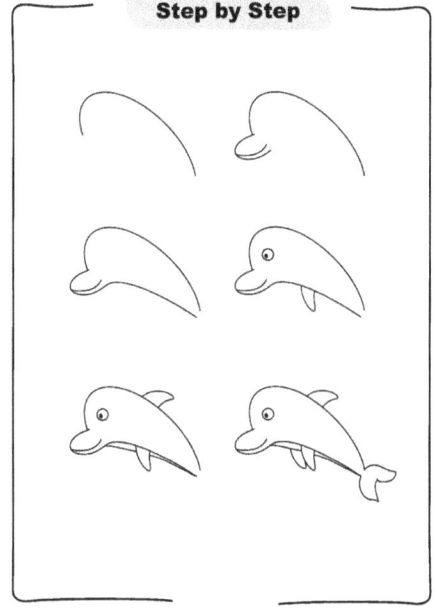

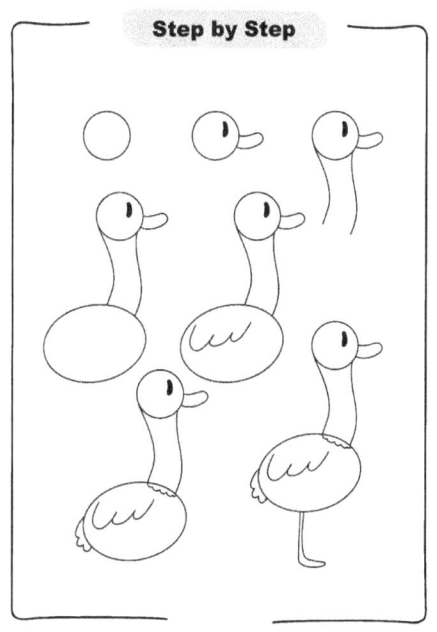

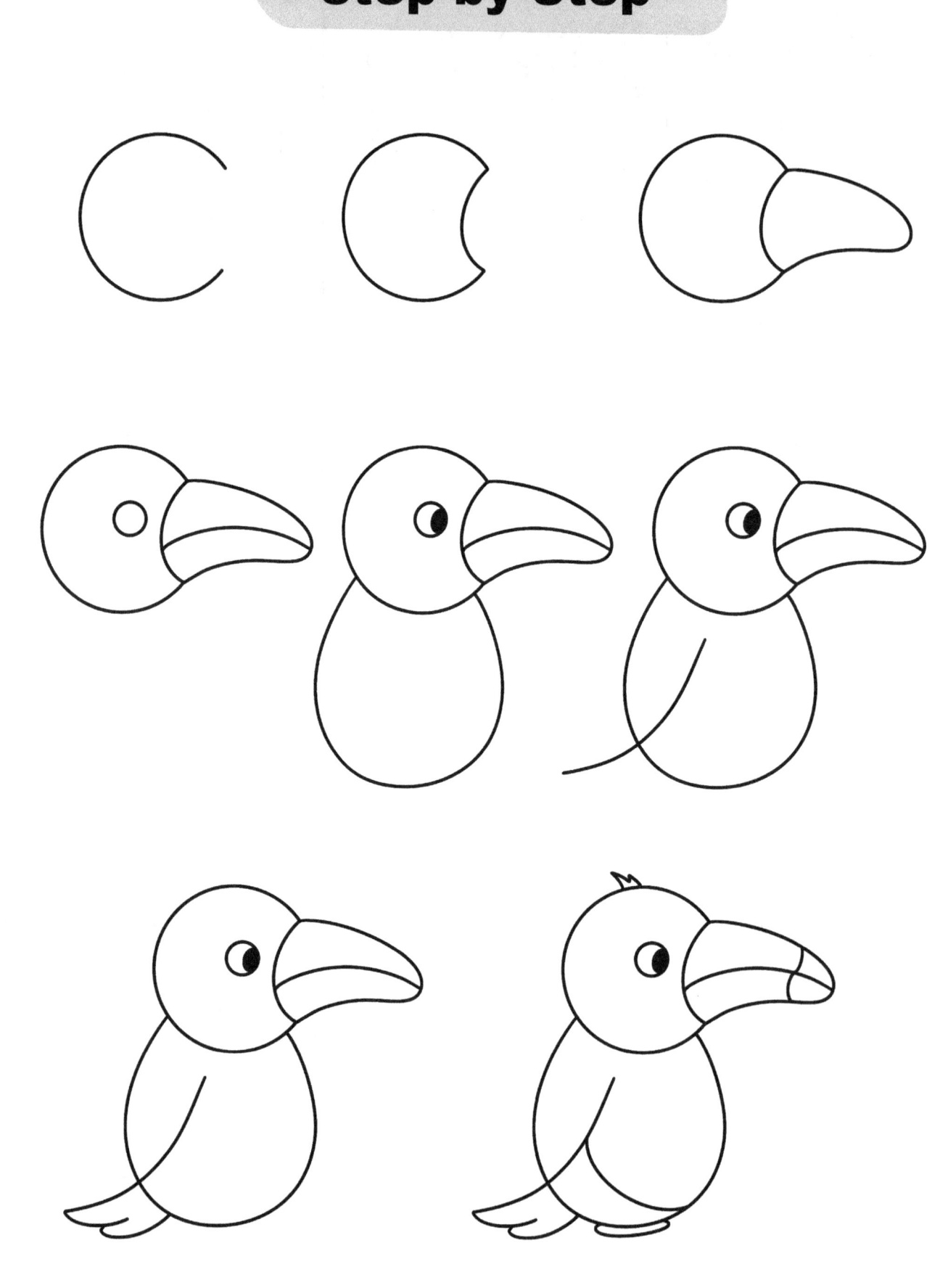

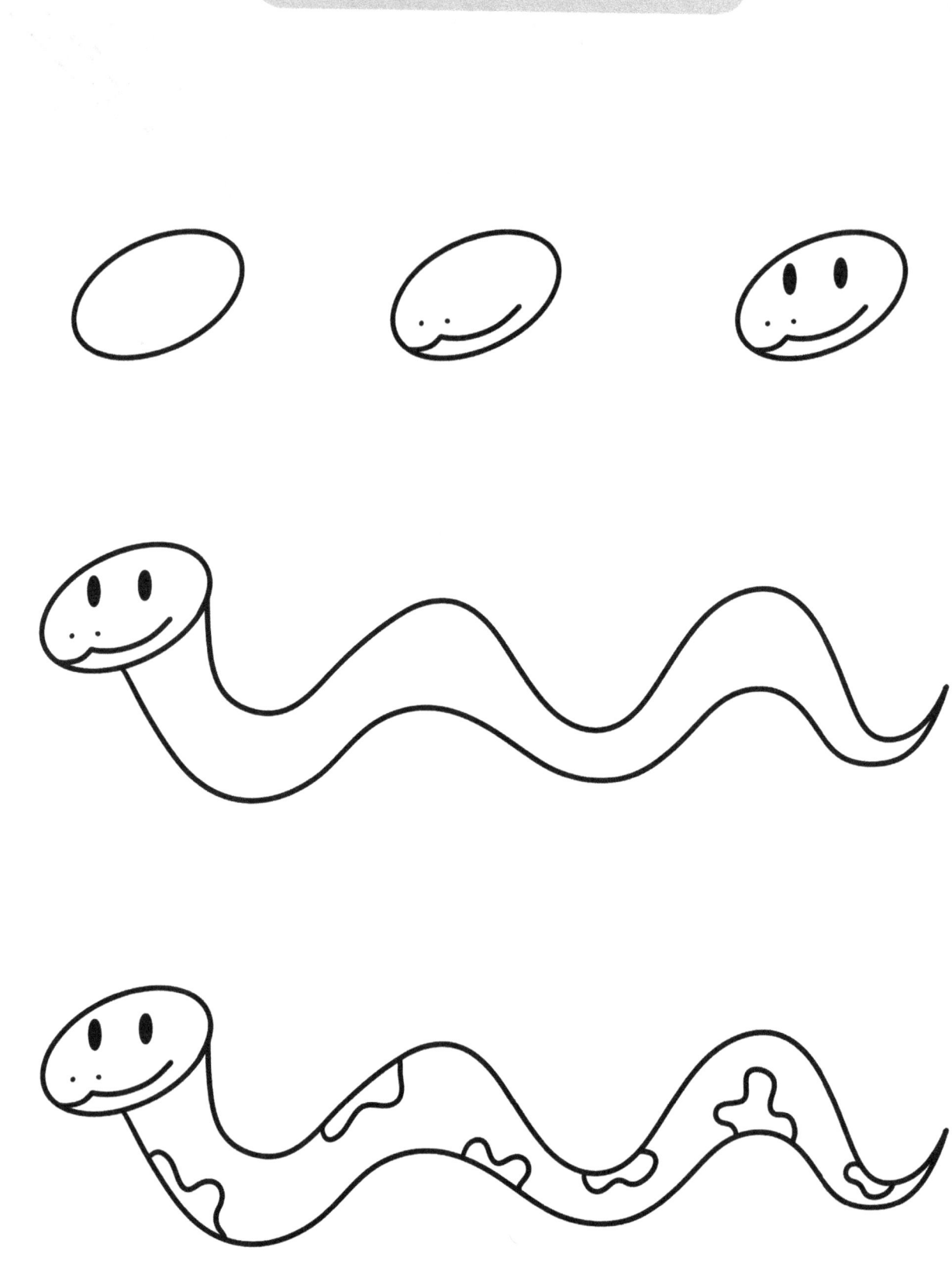

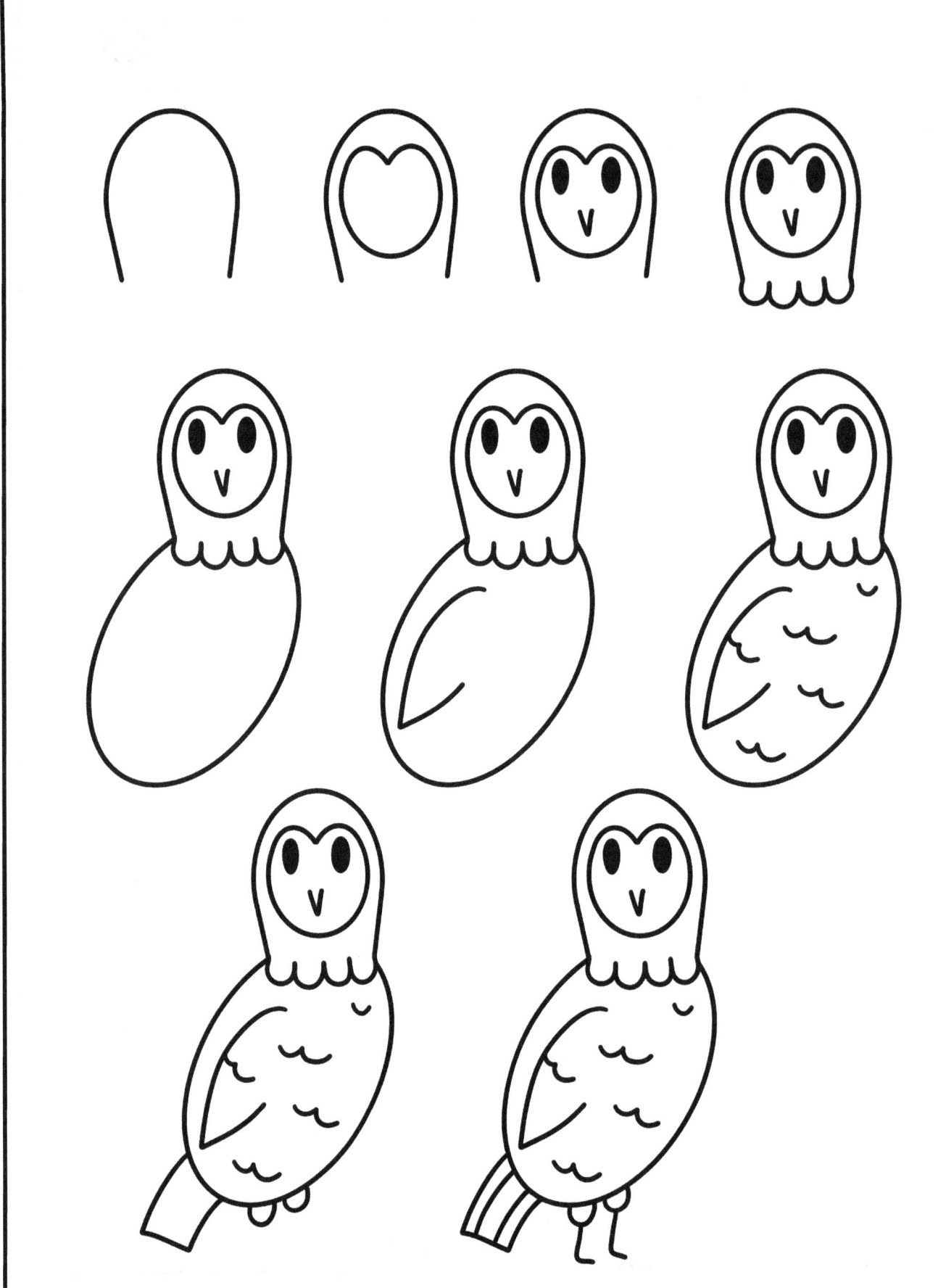

Step by Step

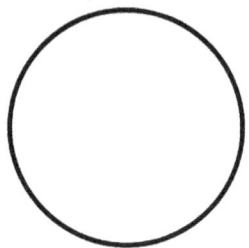
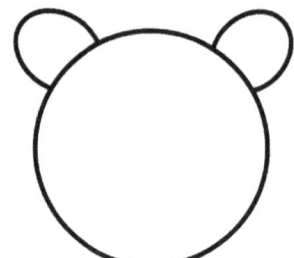
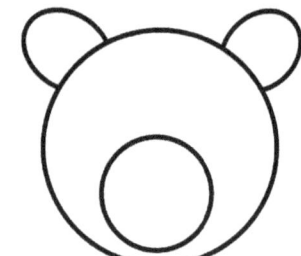
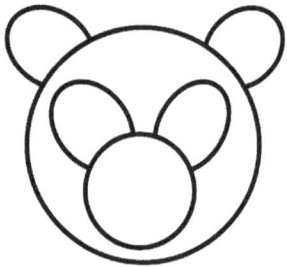
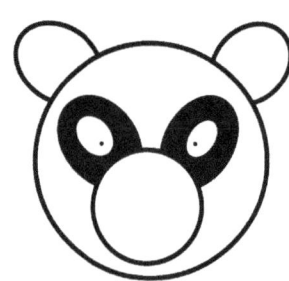
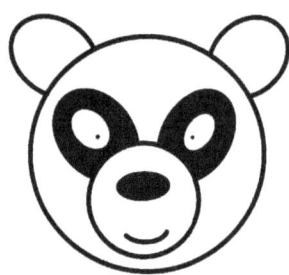
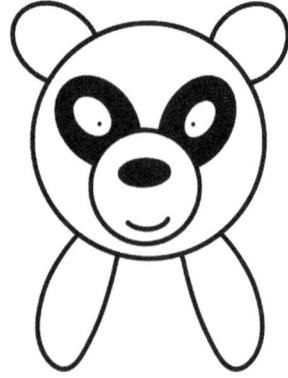
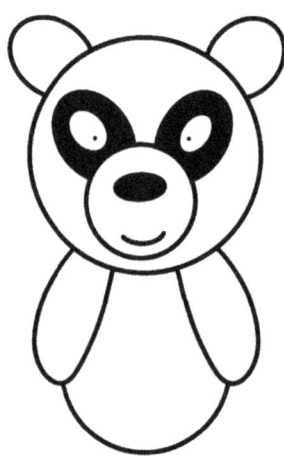
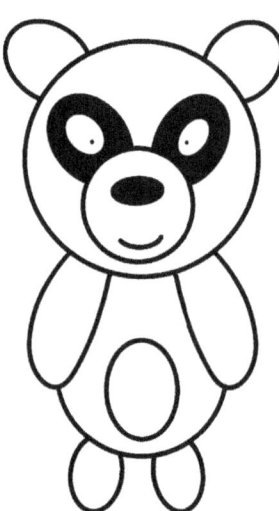

Step by Step

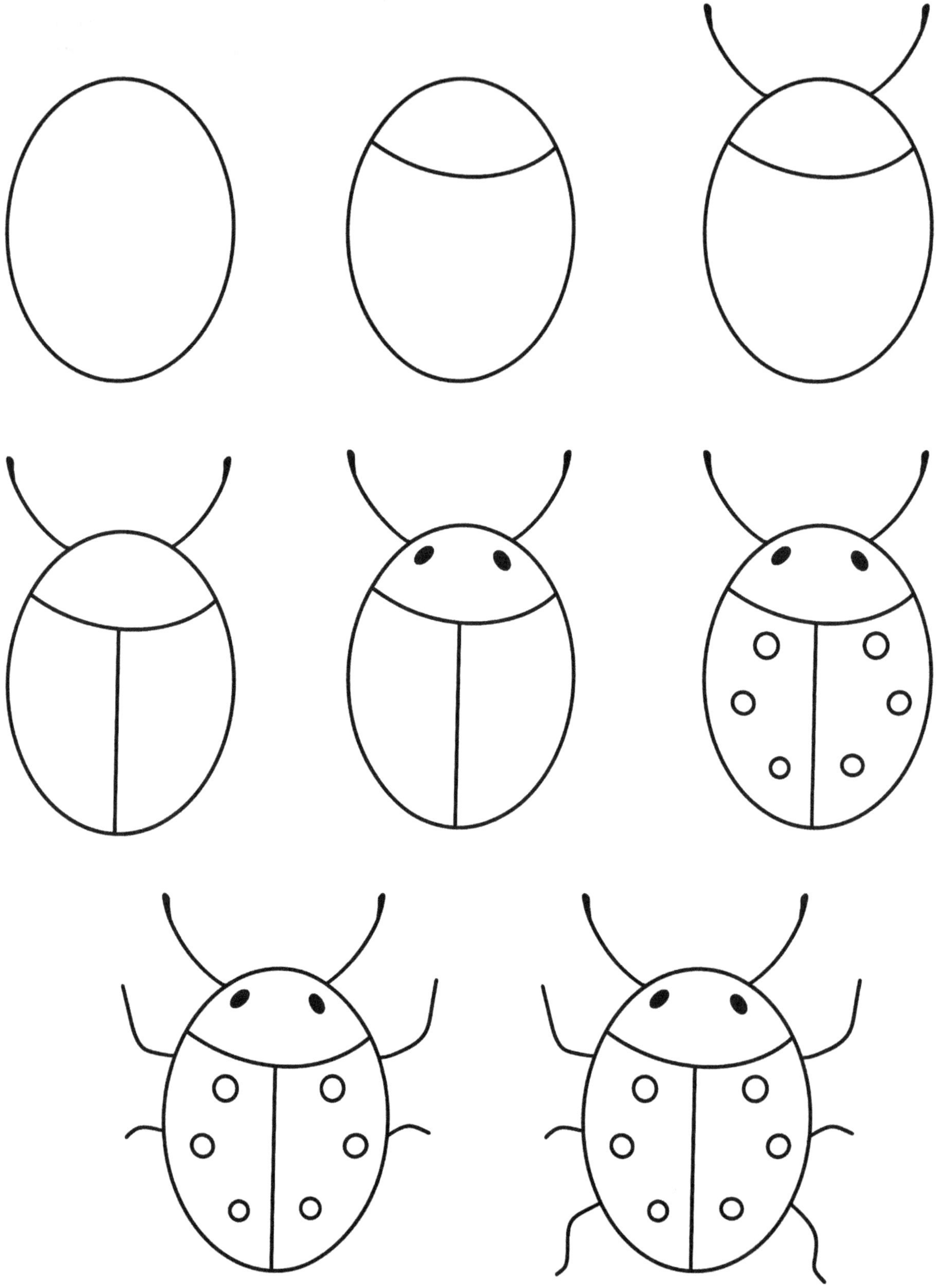

It's your turn

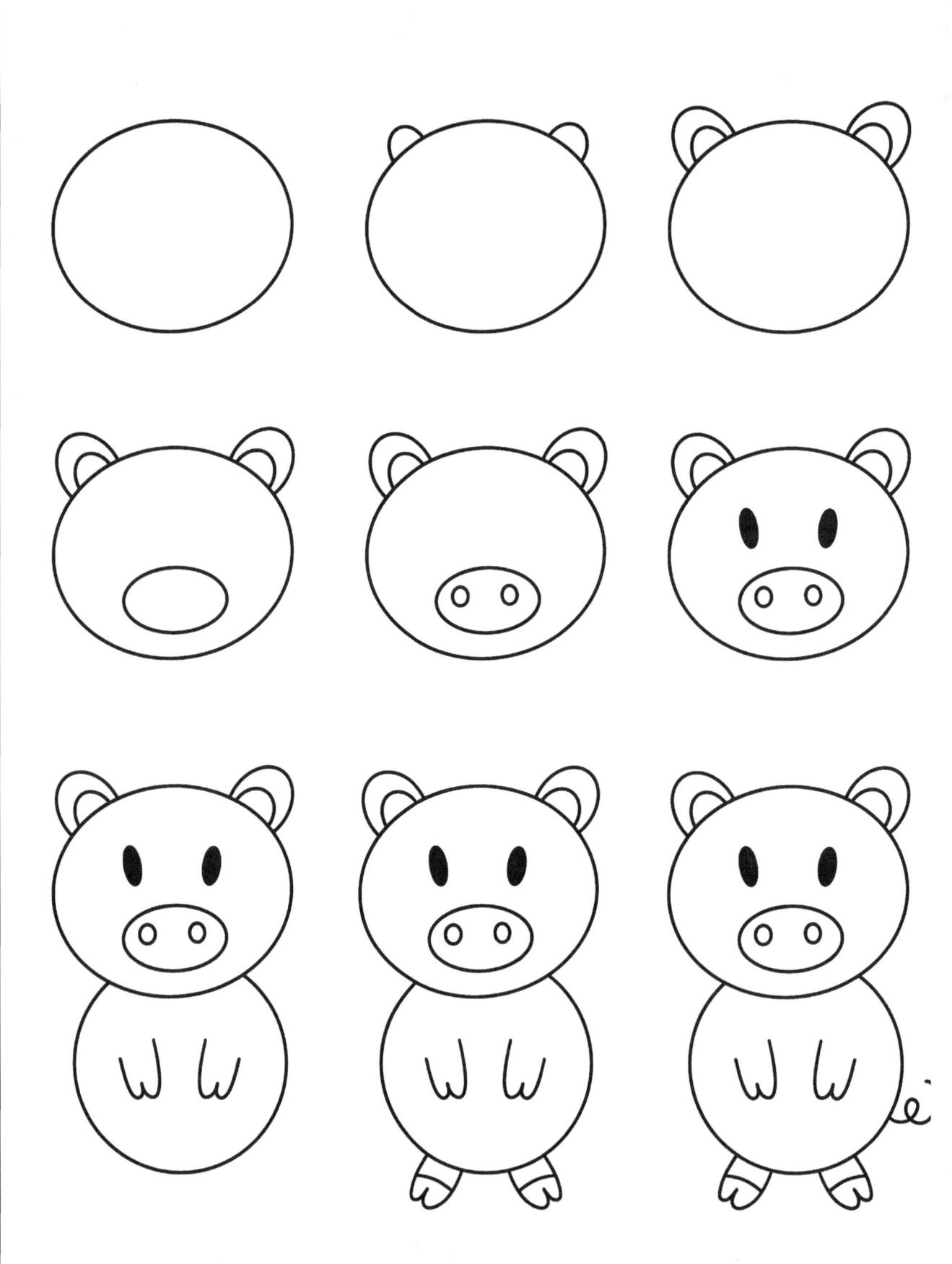

Step by Step

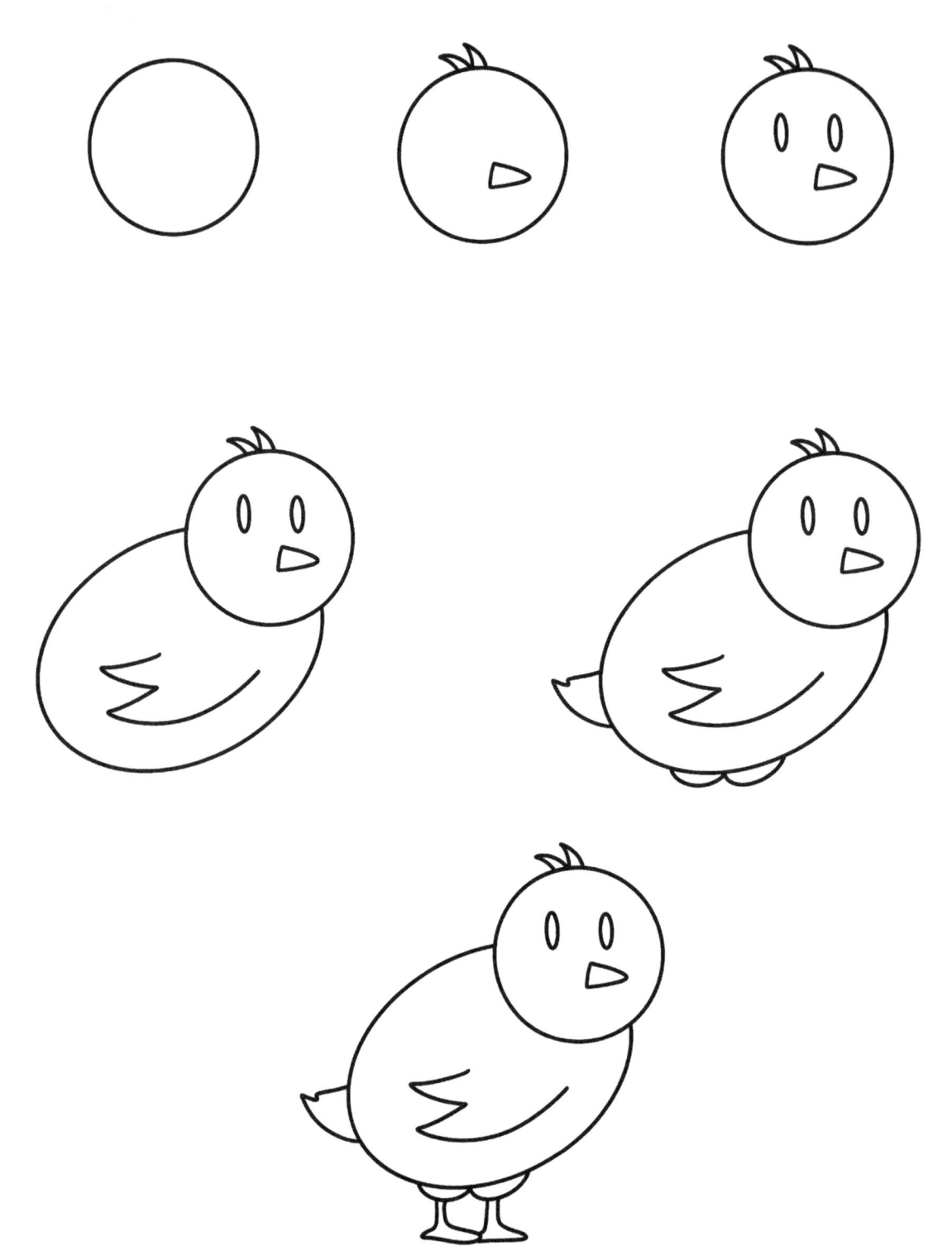

It's your turn

Step by Step

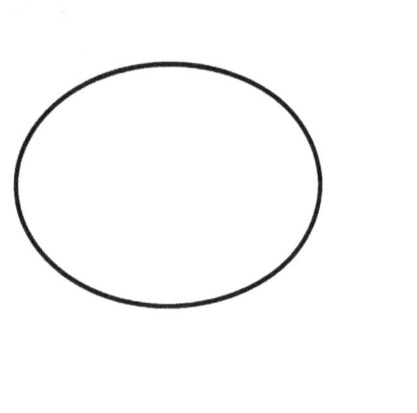 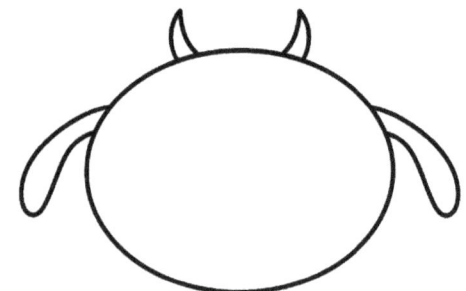

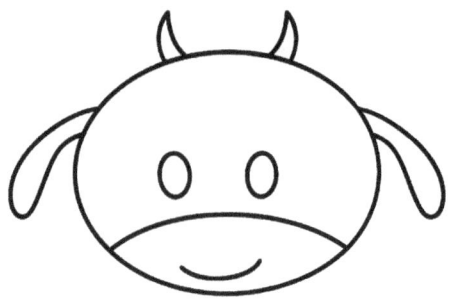 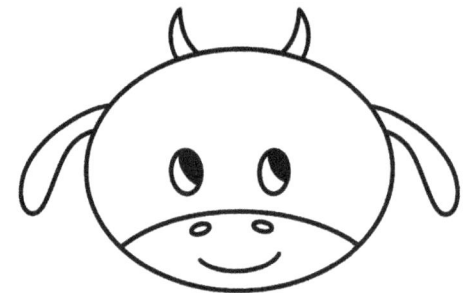

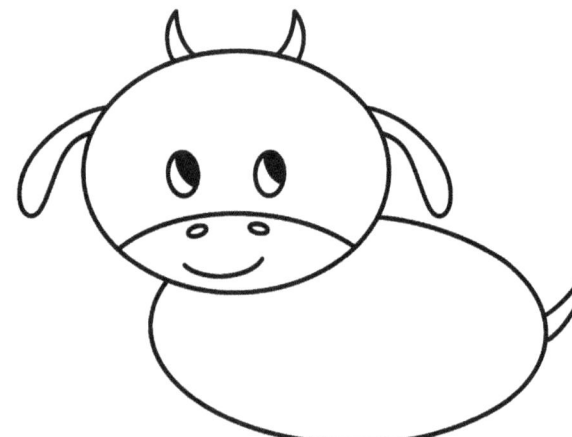 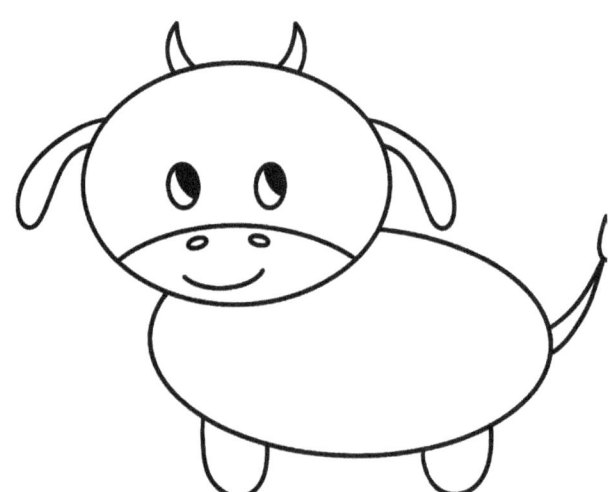

Step by Step

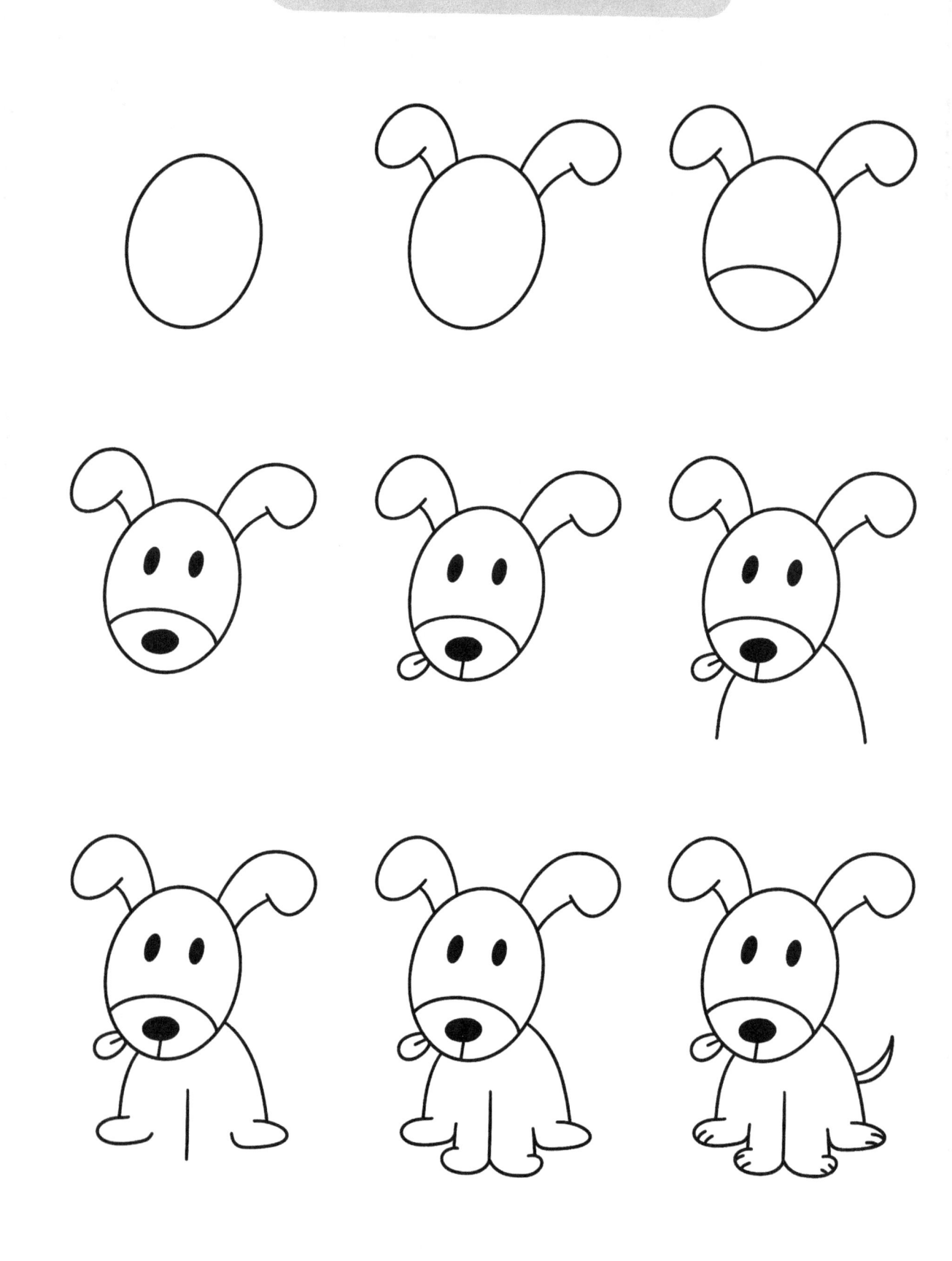

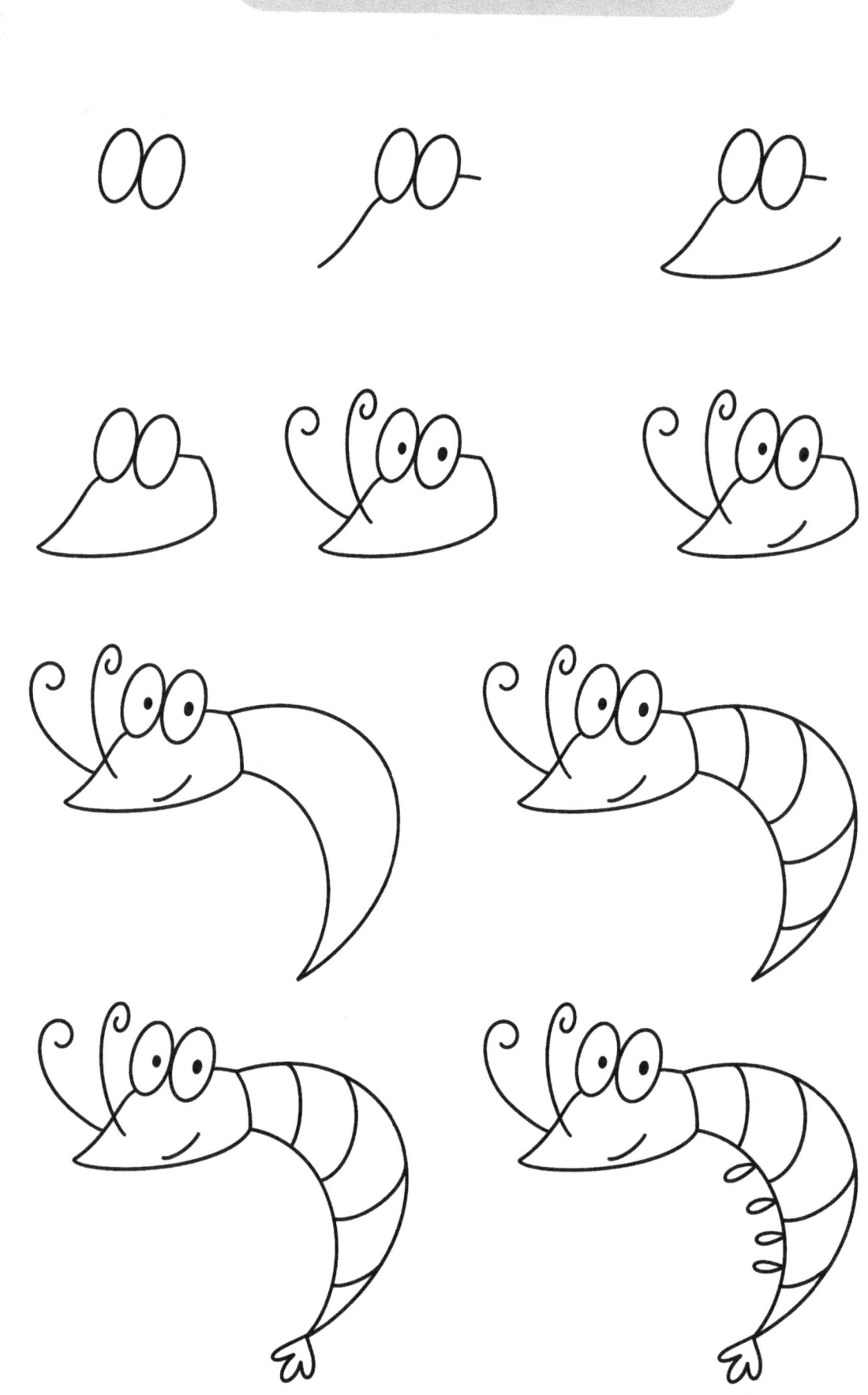

Step by Step

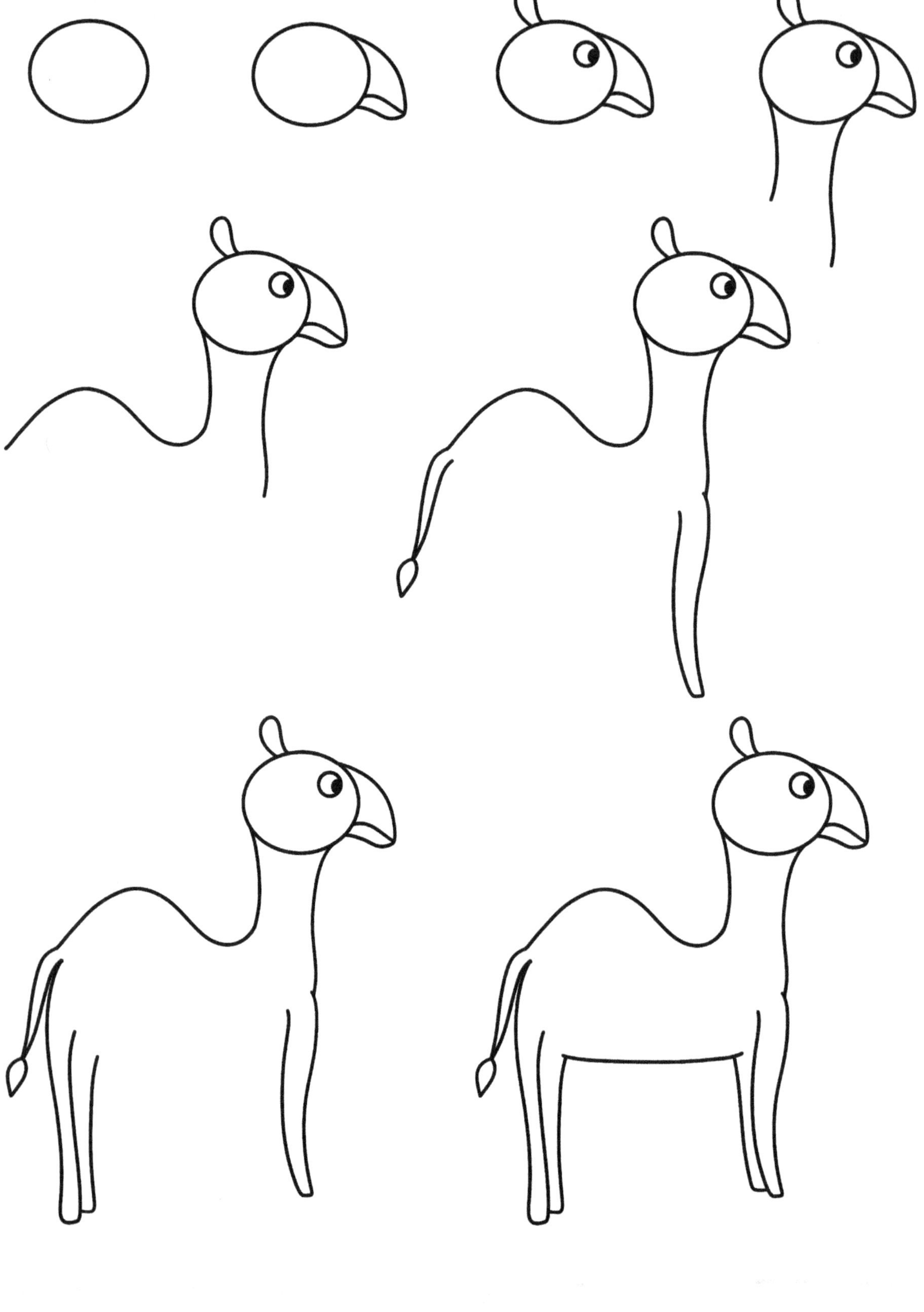

Step by Step

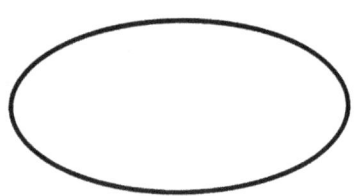
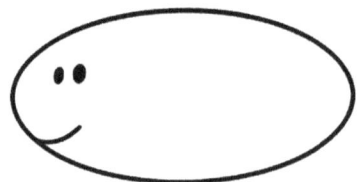

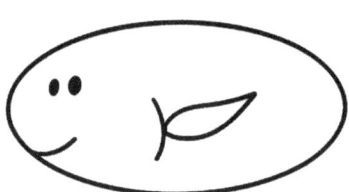
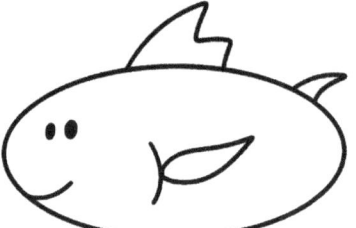

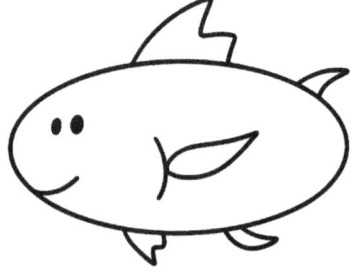
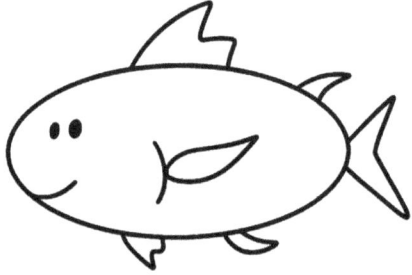

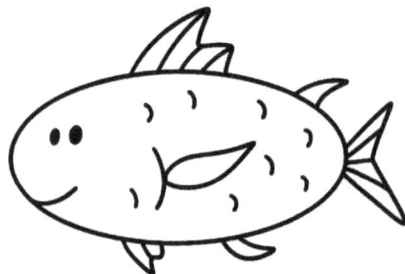

Step by Step

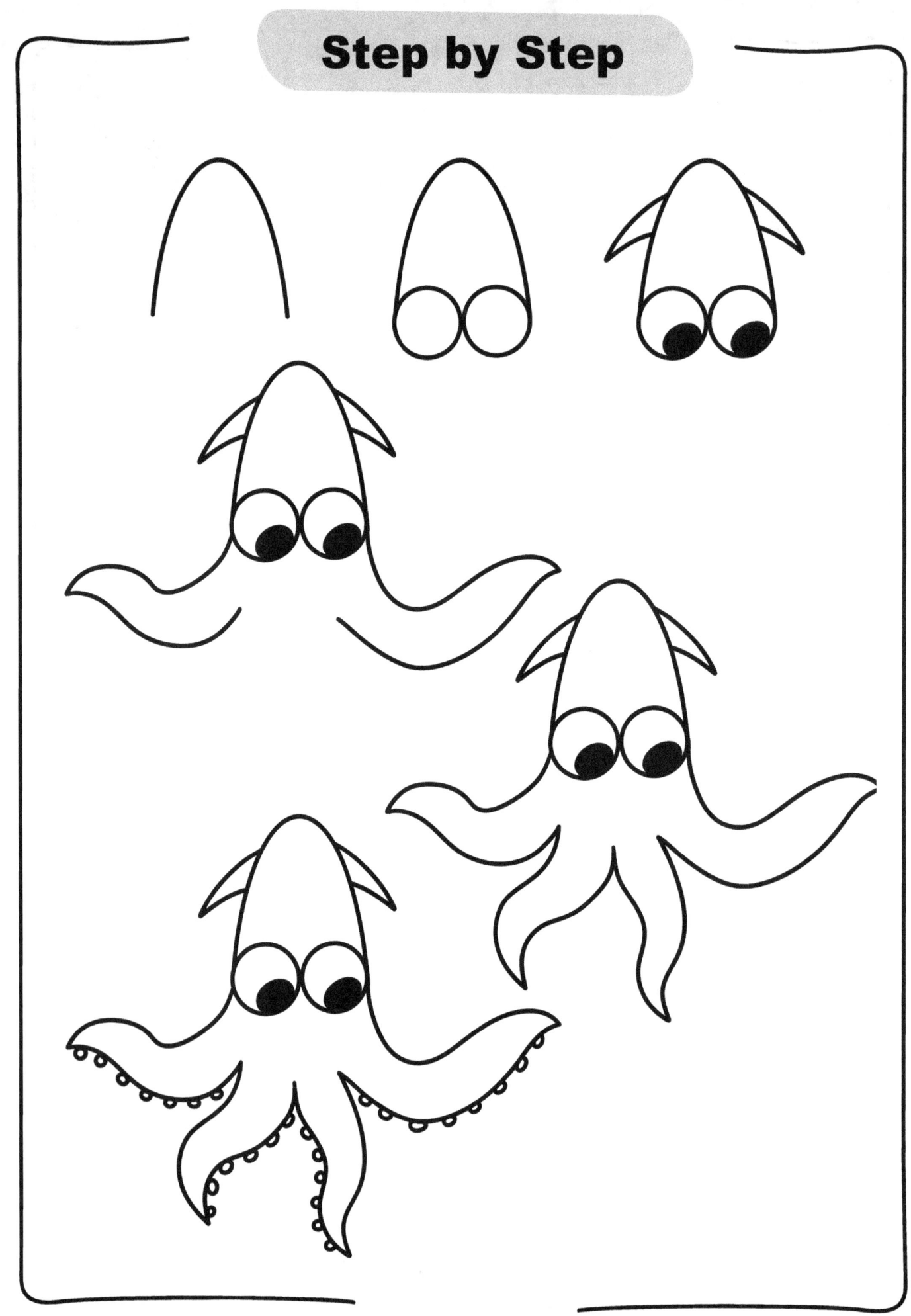

Step by Step

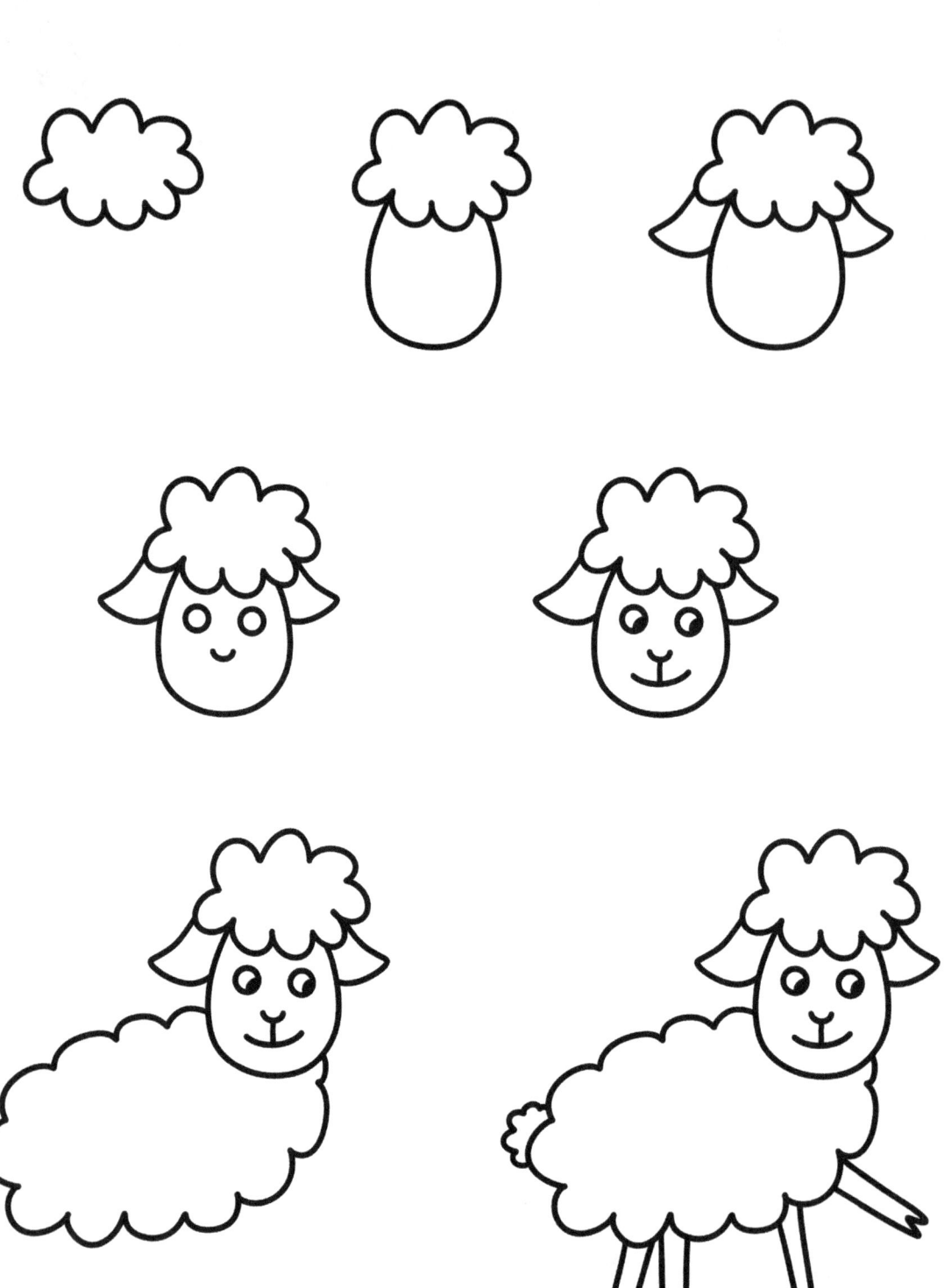

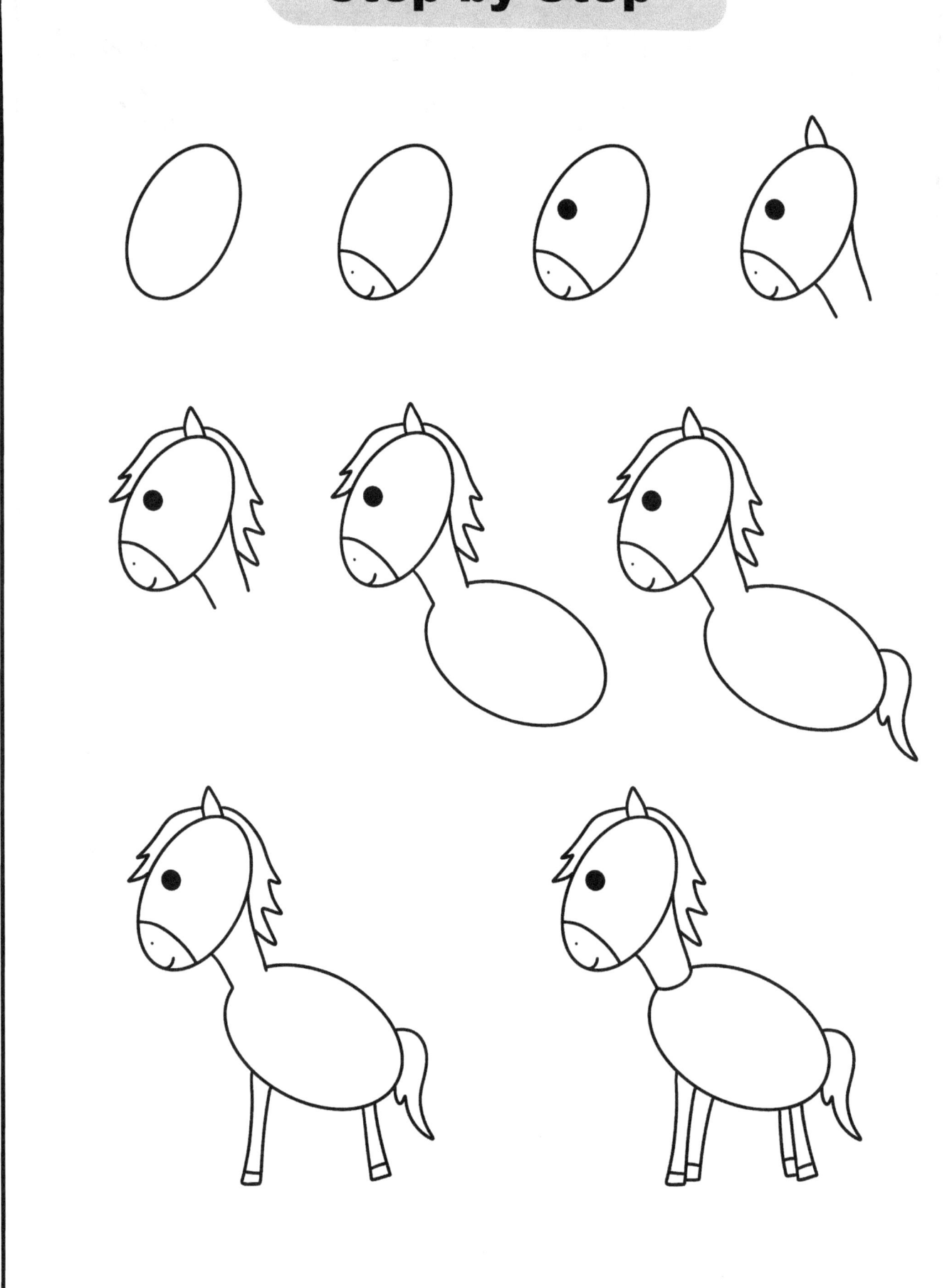

Step by Step

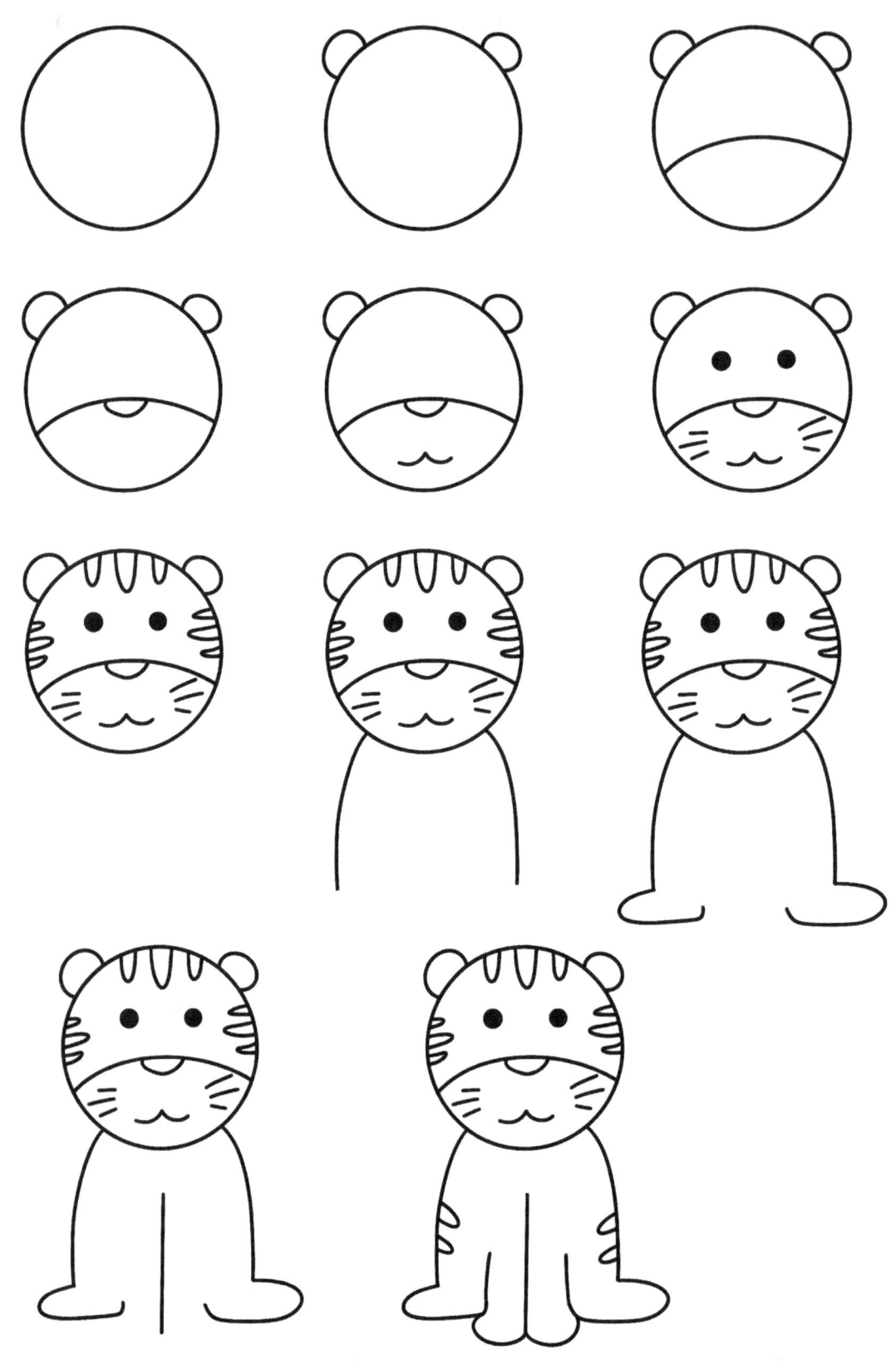

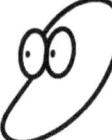
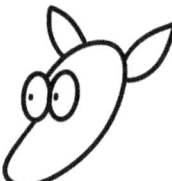
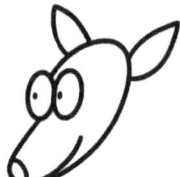

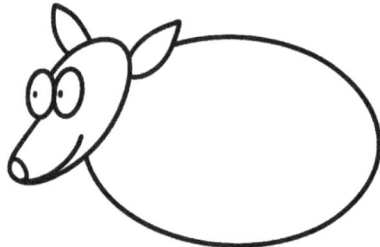
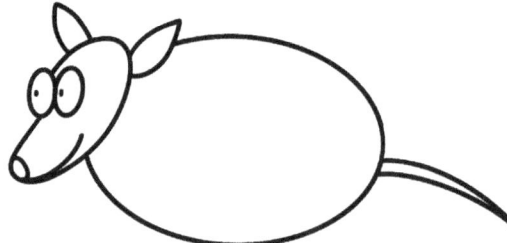

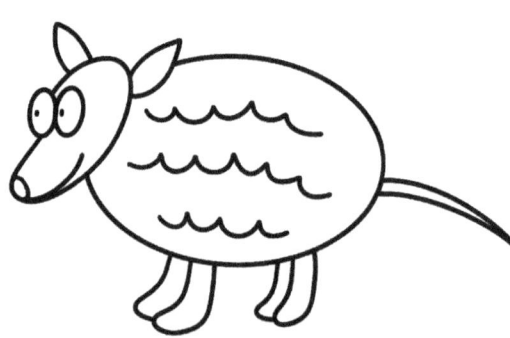

It's your turn

Step by Step

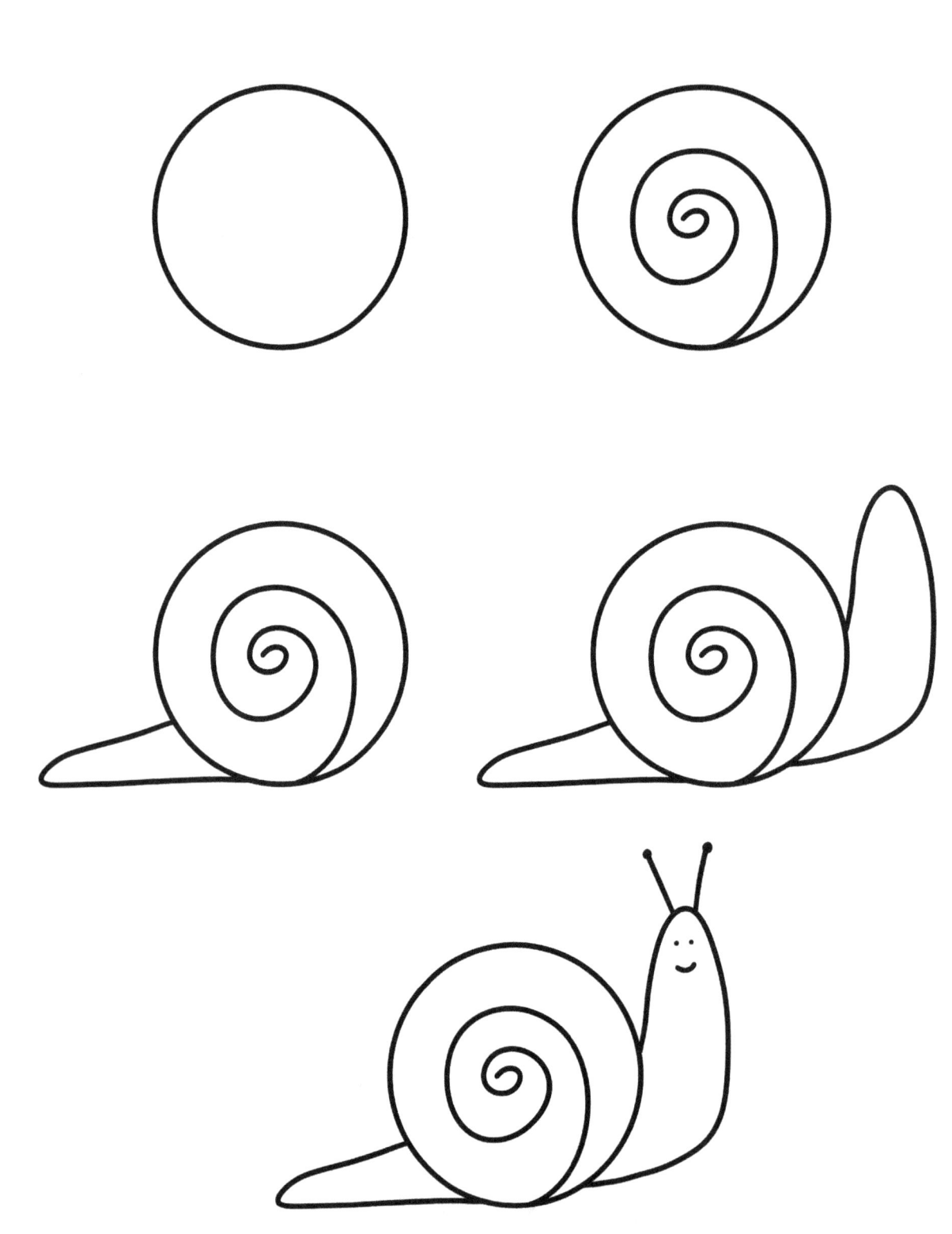

It's your turn

Step by Step

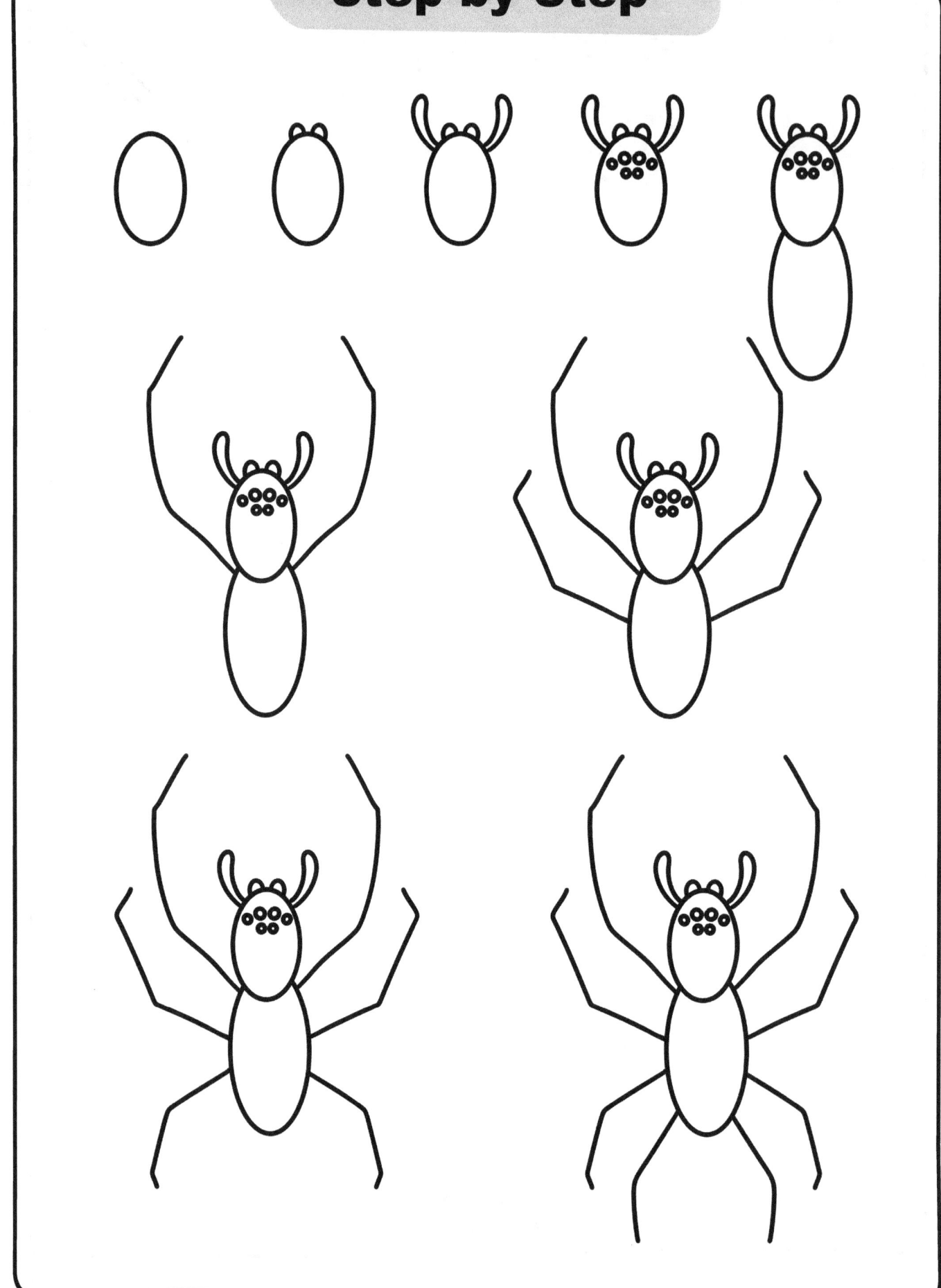

Step by Step

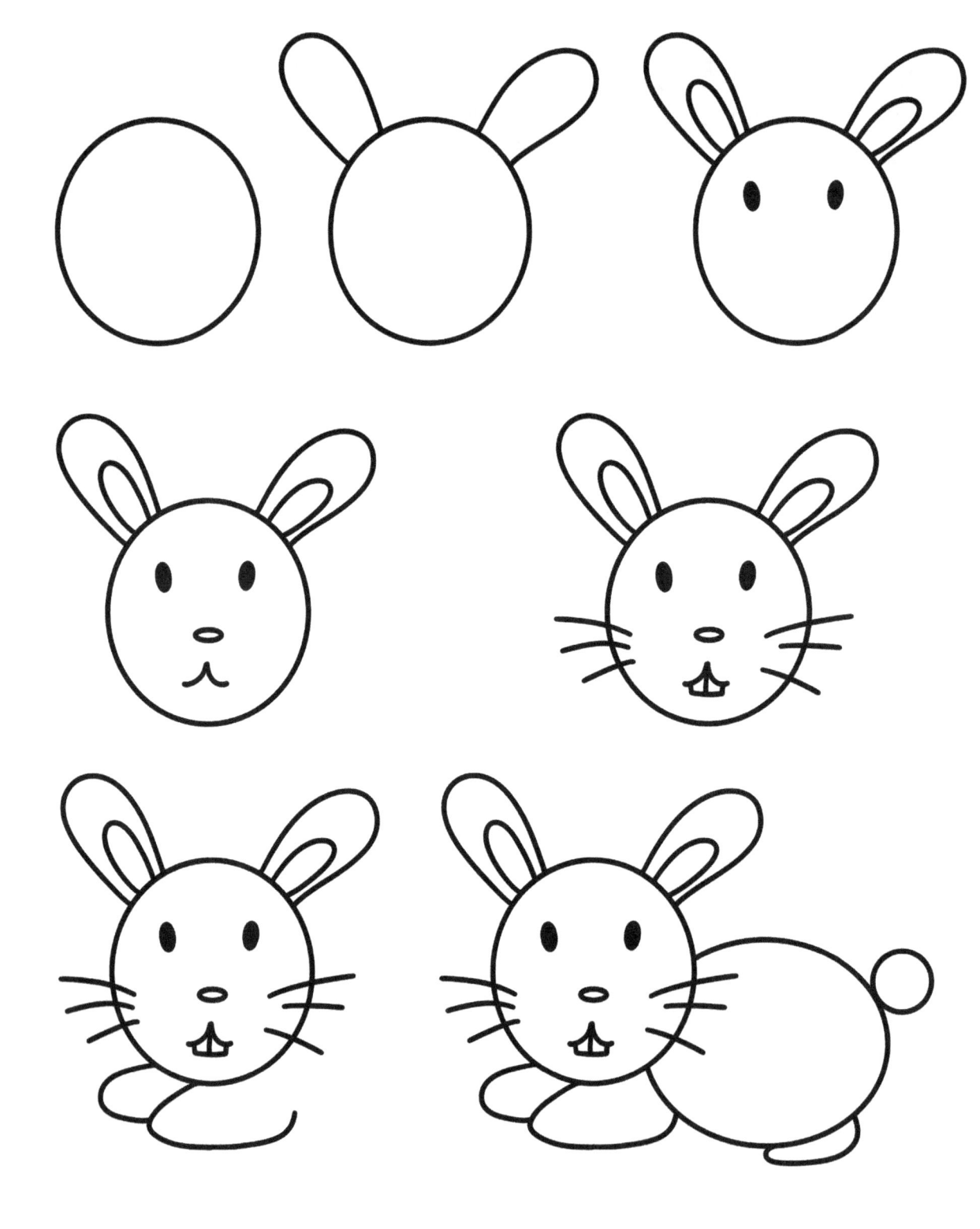

Step by Step

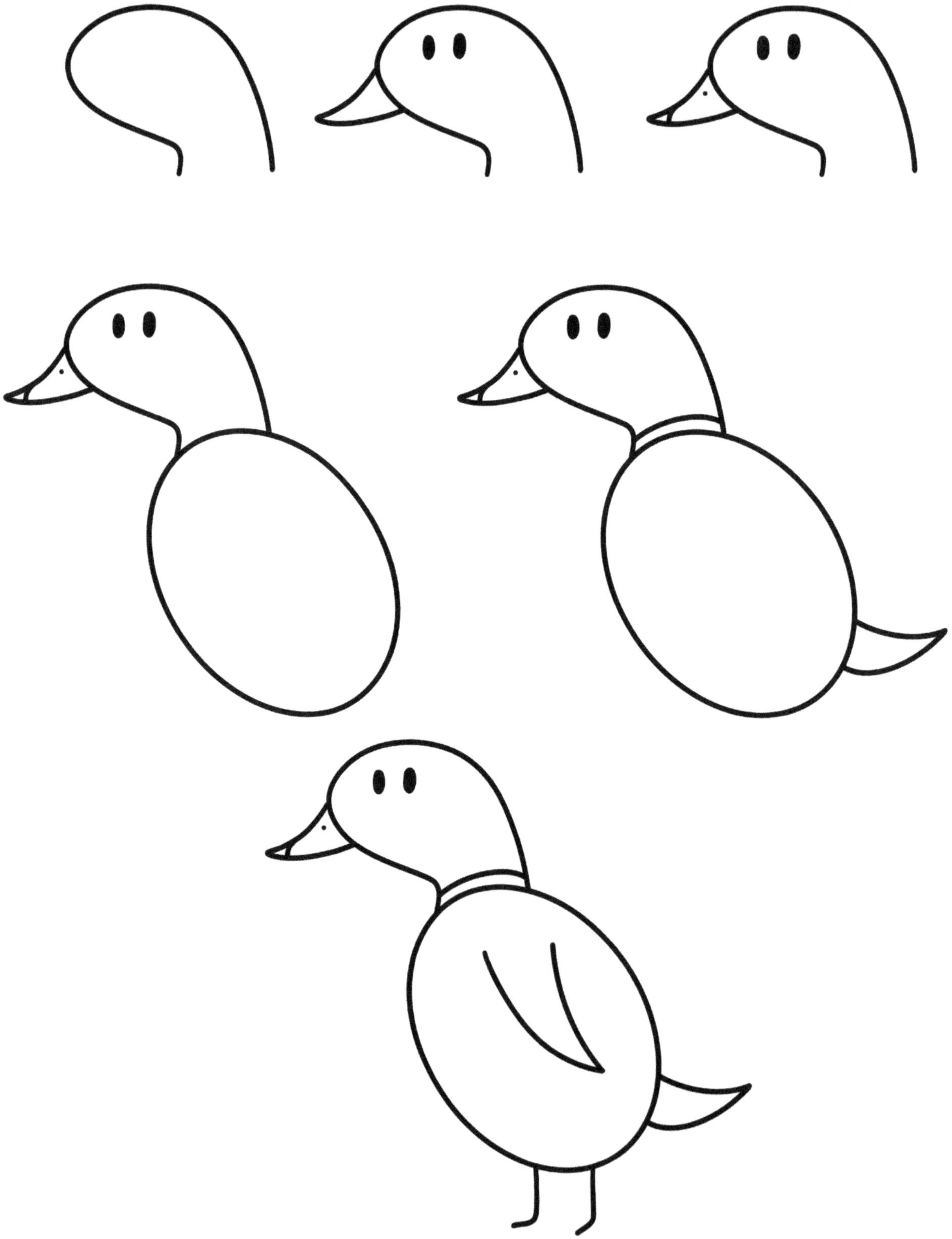

Step by Step

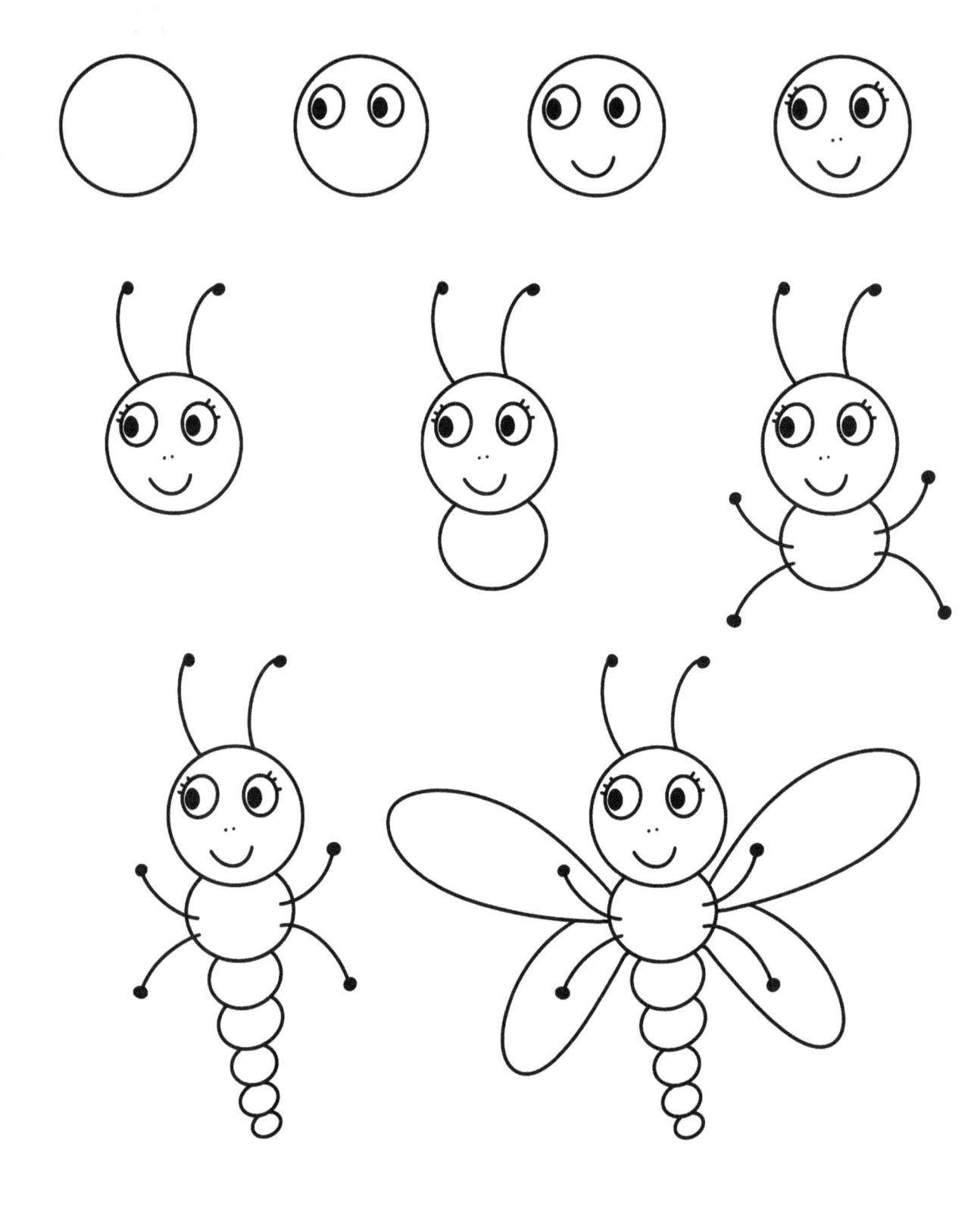

Step by Step

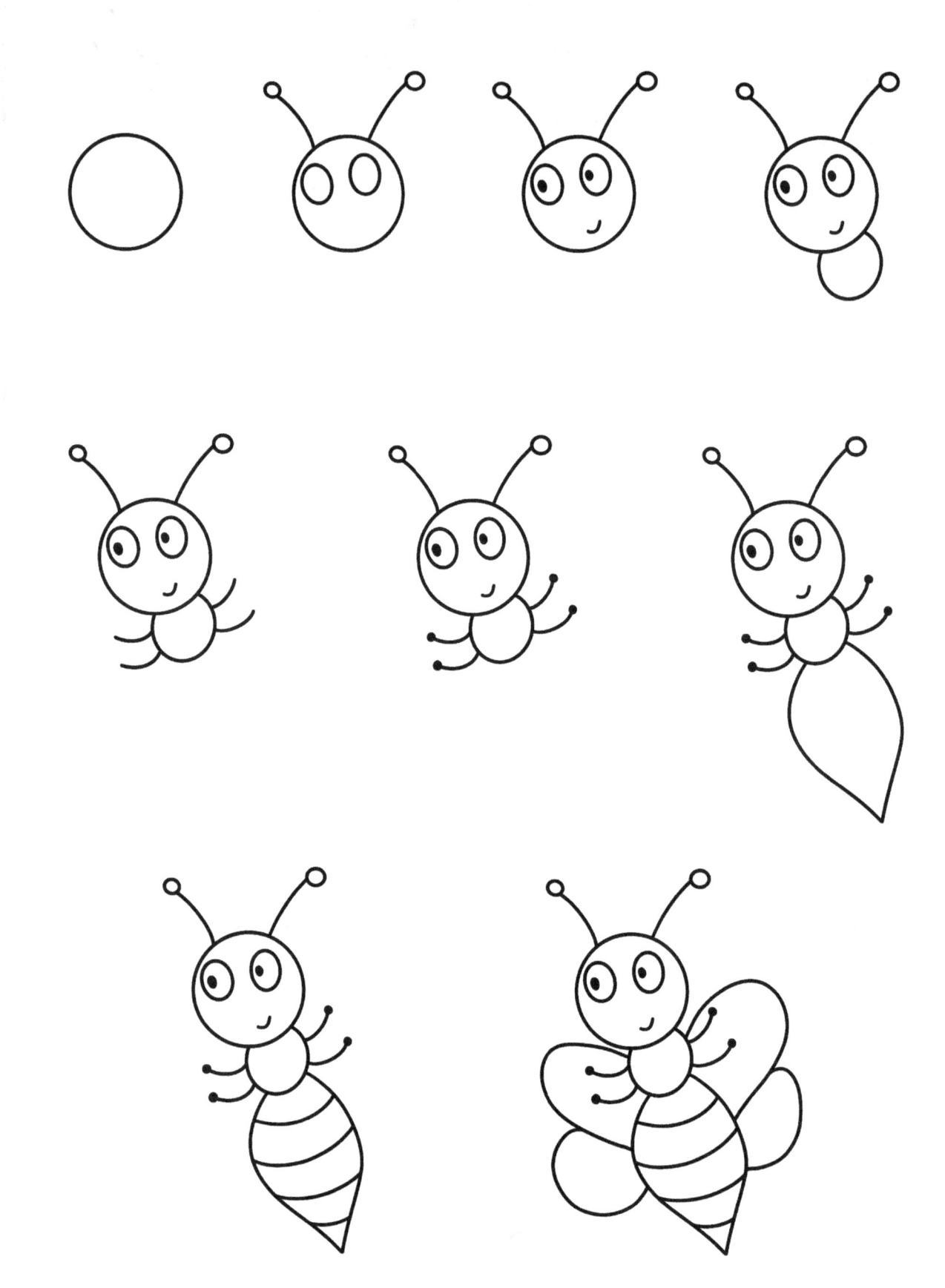

Step by Step

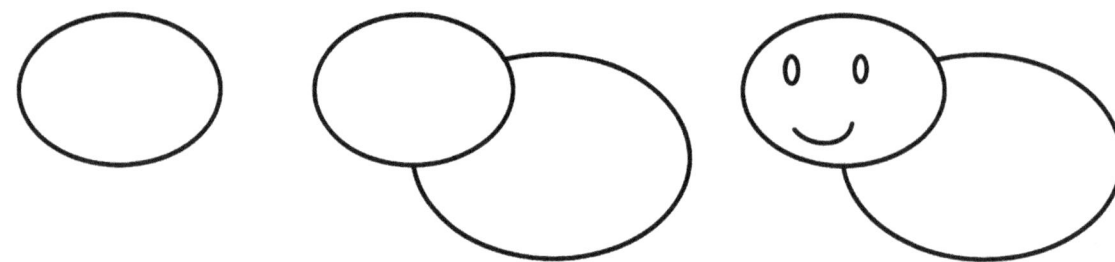

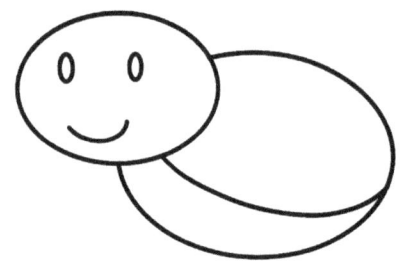

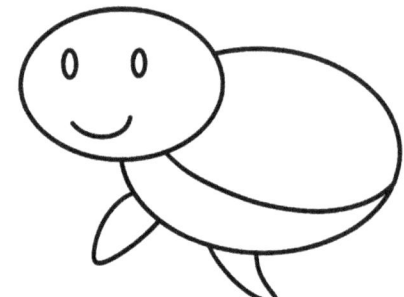

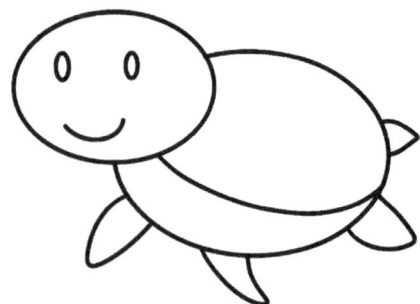

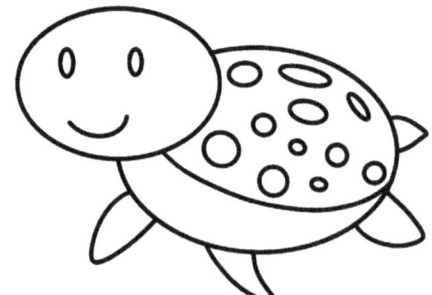

Step by Step

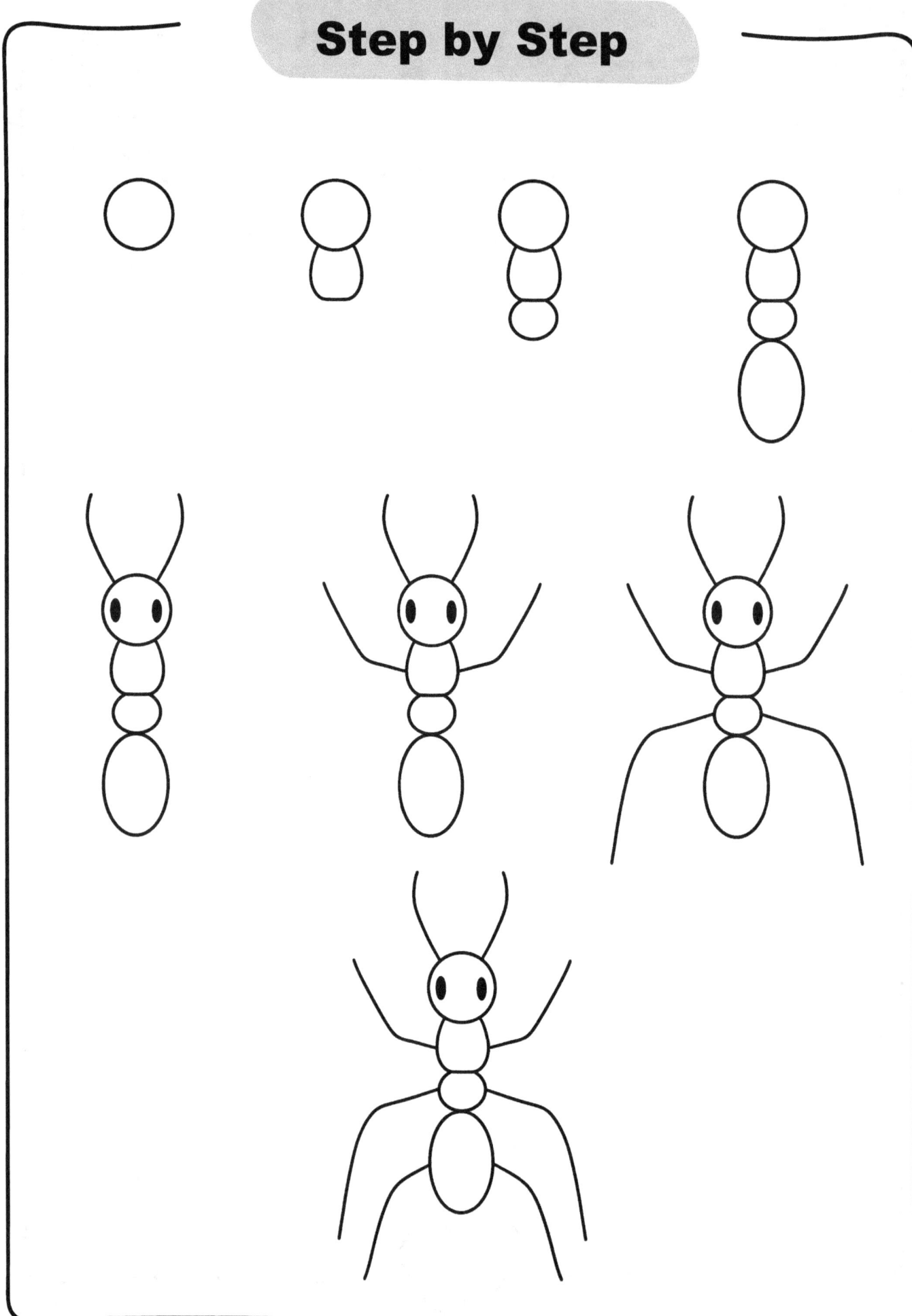

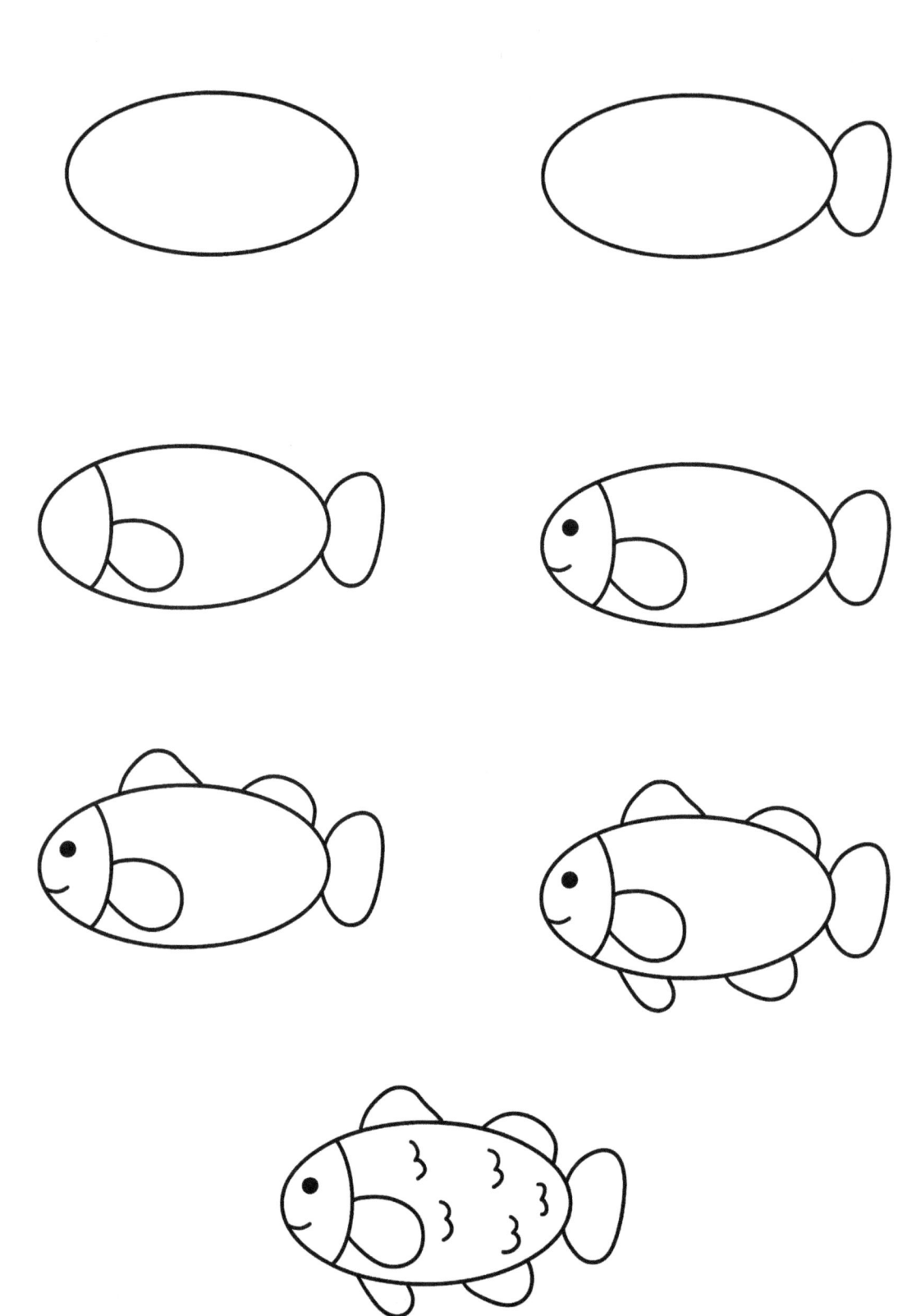

Step by Step

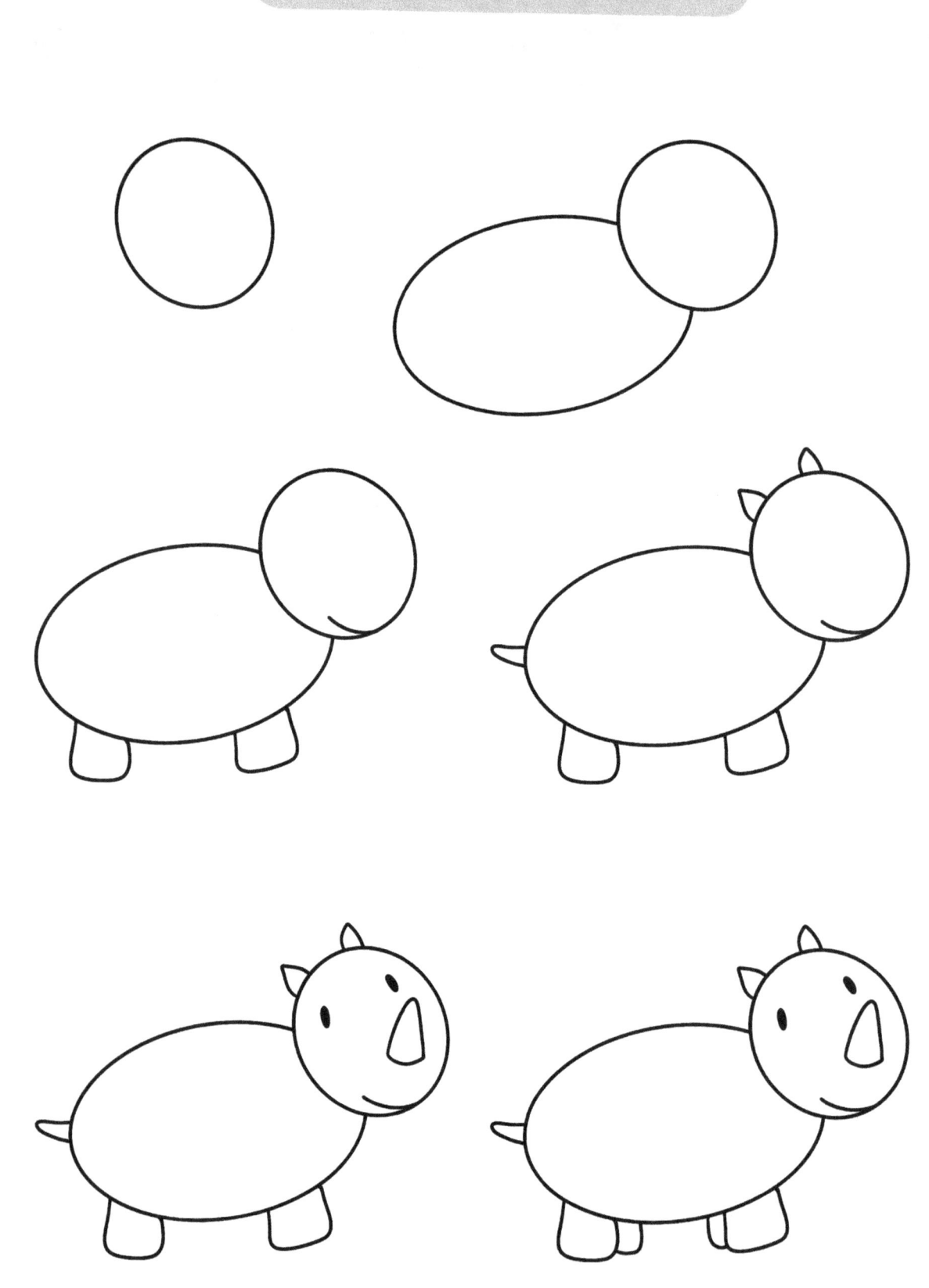

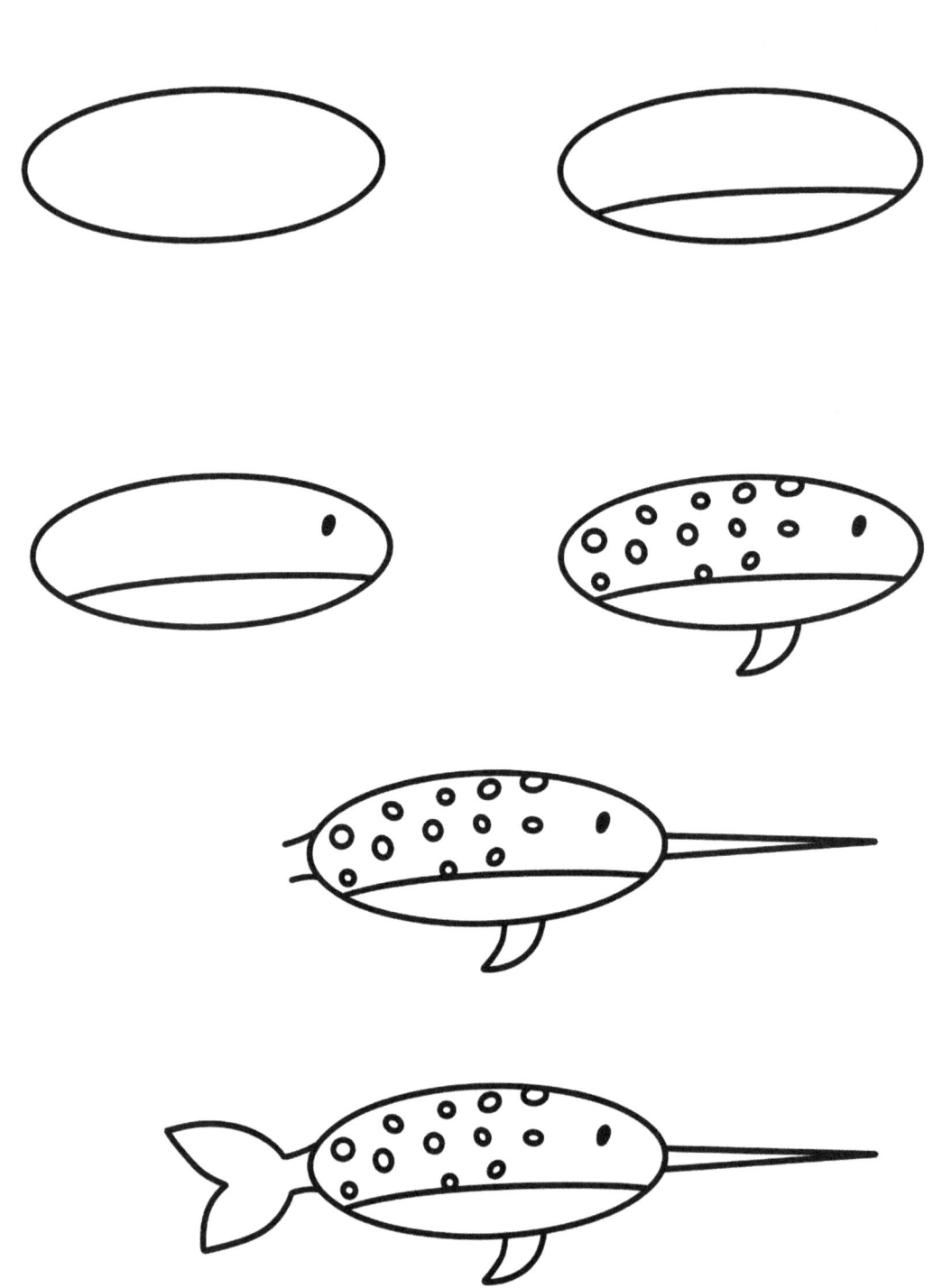

Step by Step

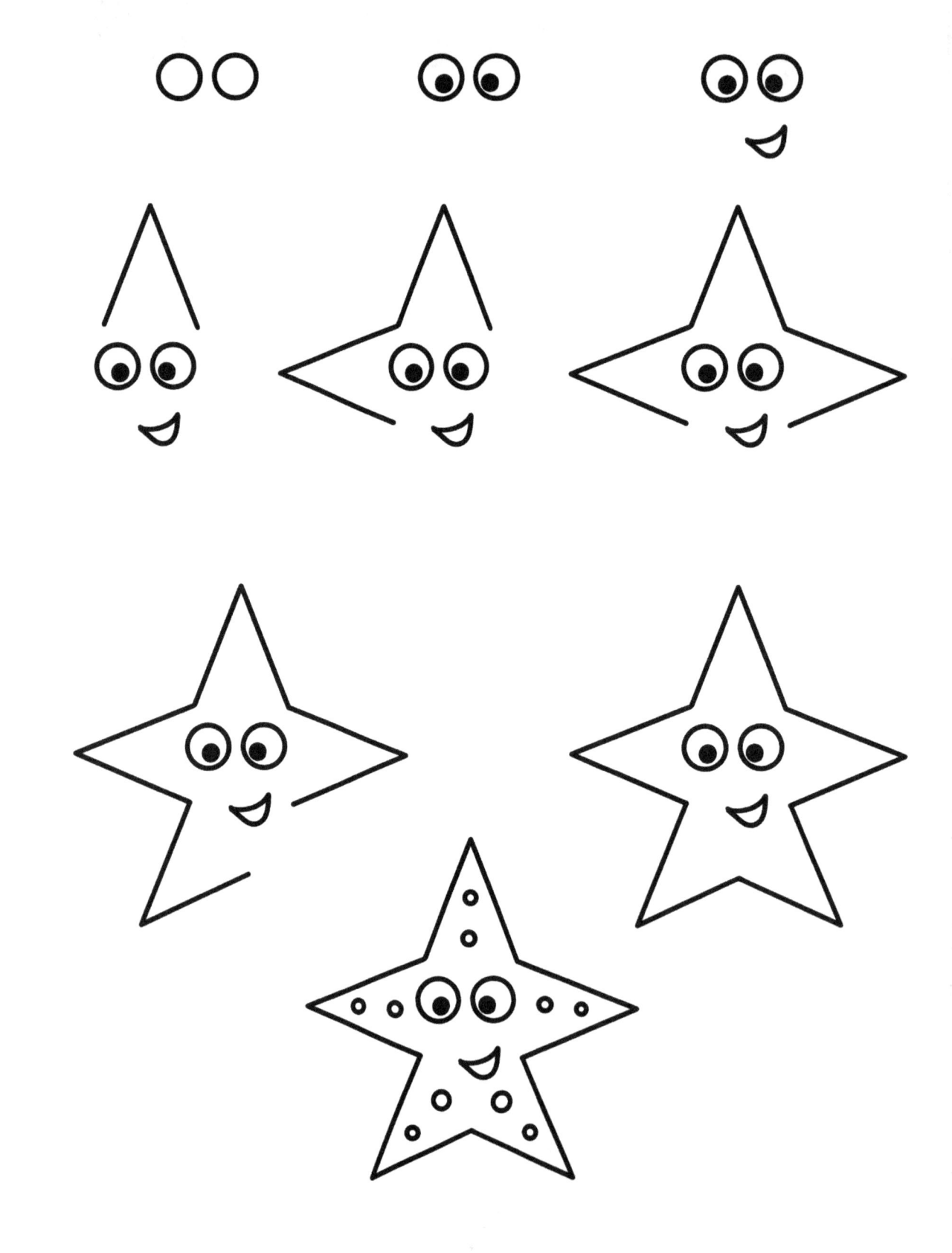

Step by Step

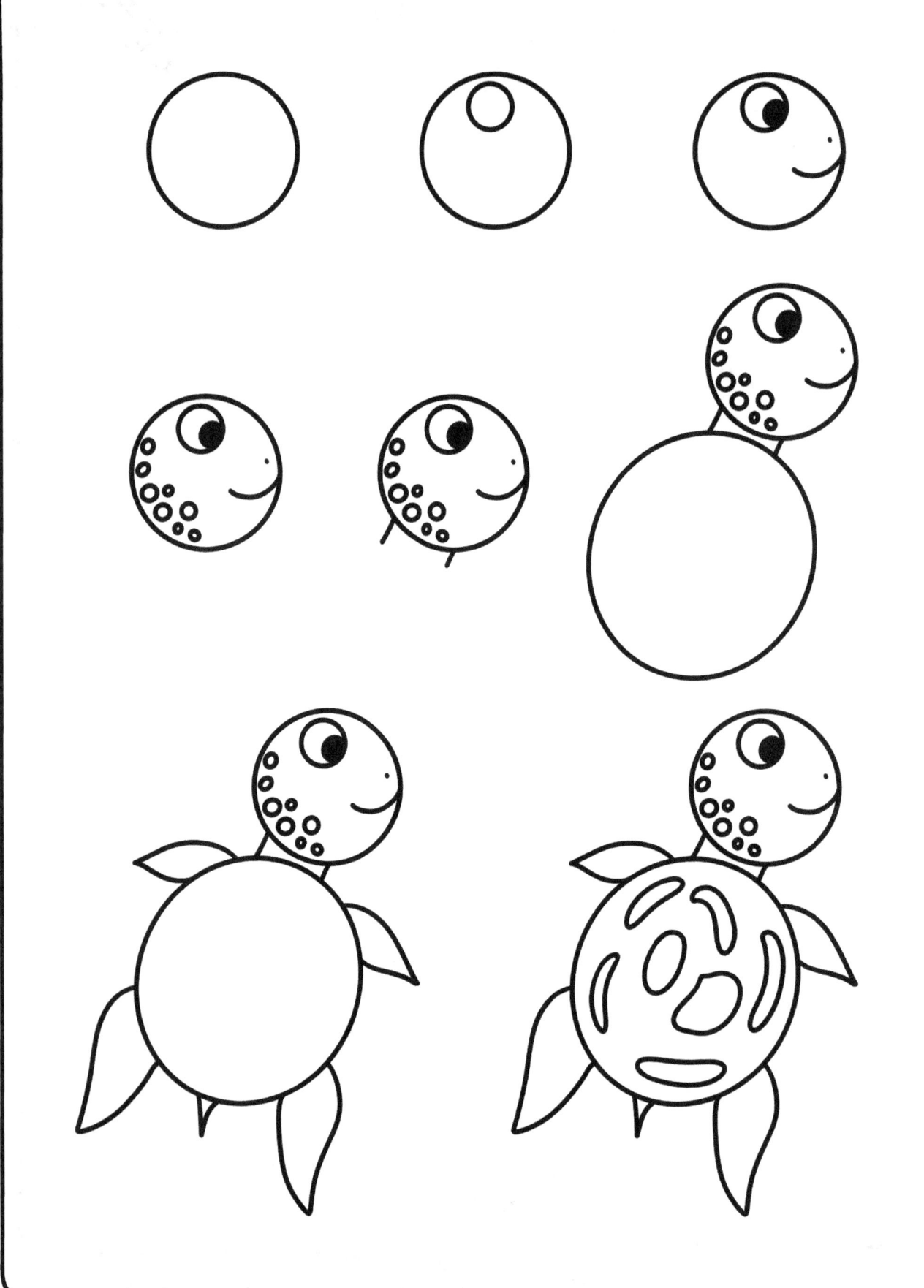

Step by Step

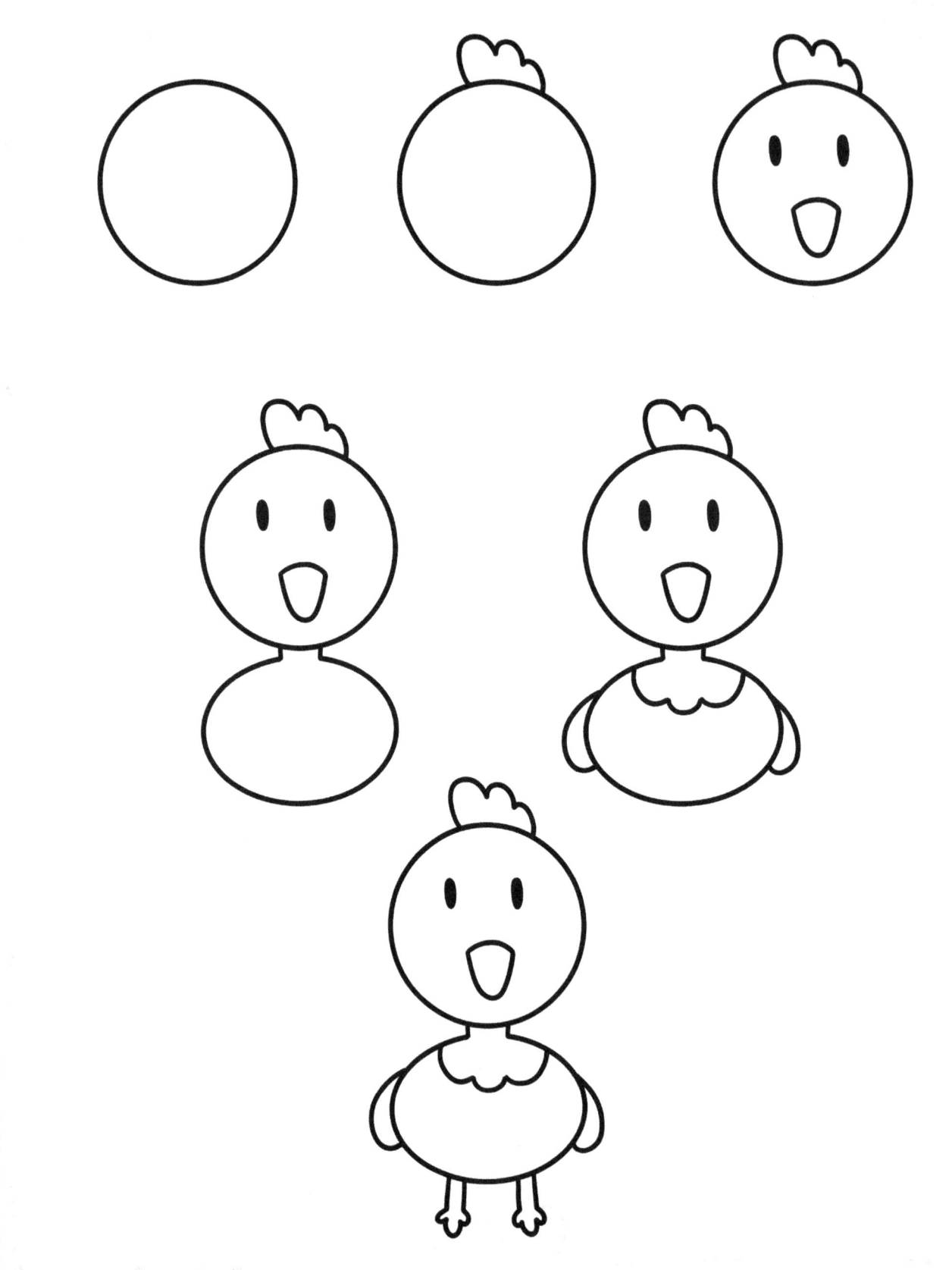

Step by Step

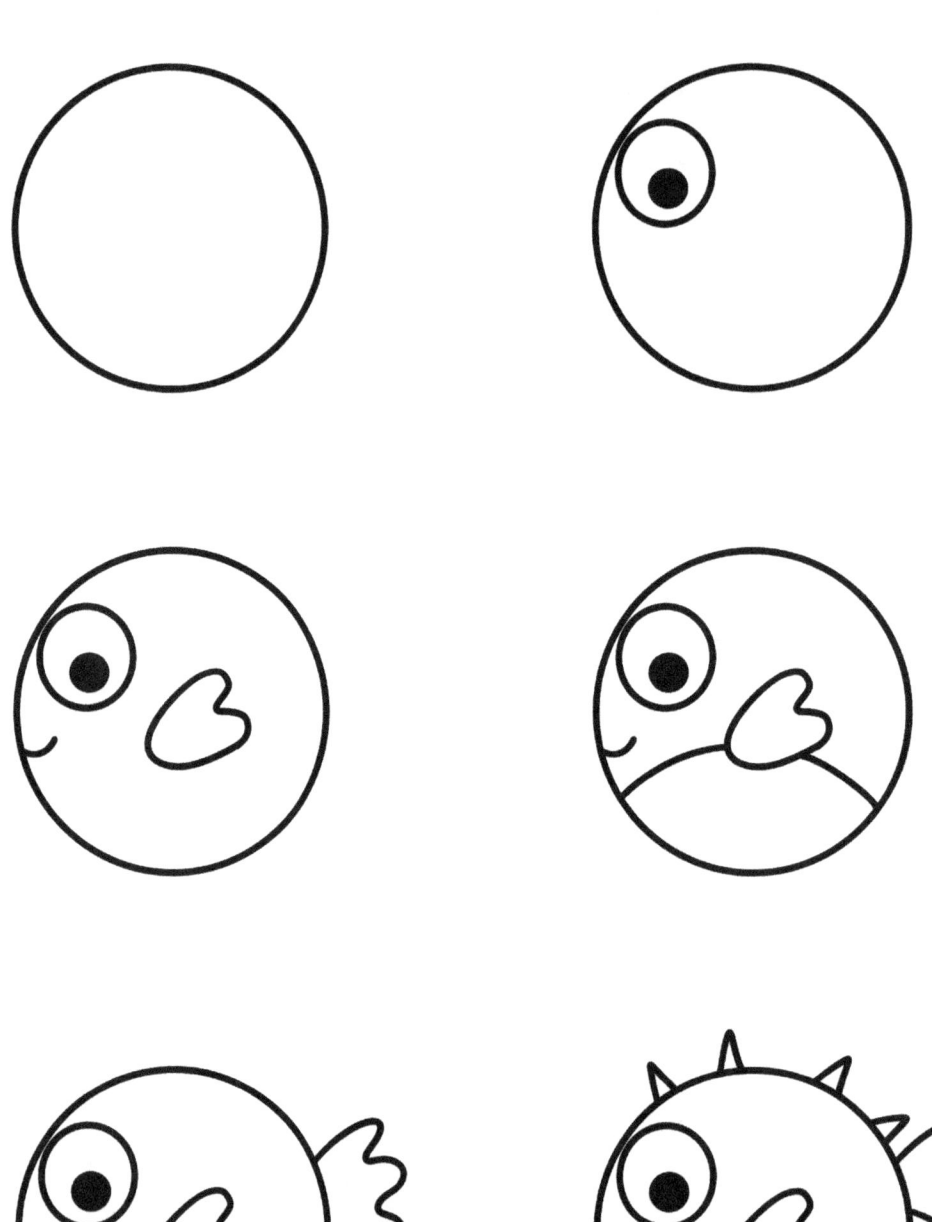

Step by Step

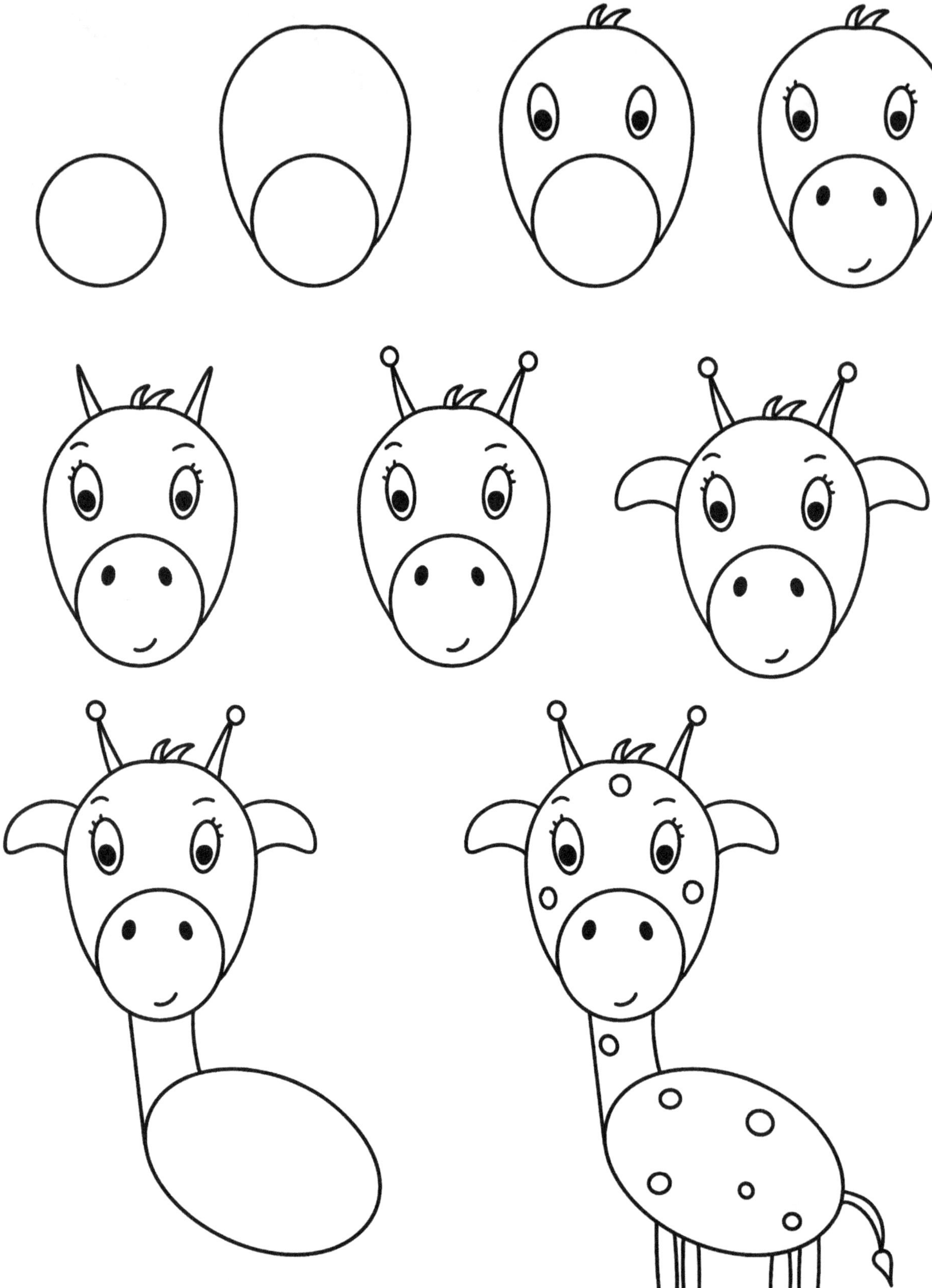

Step by Step

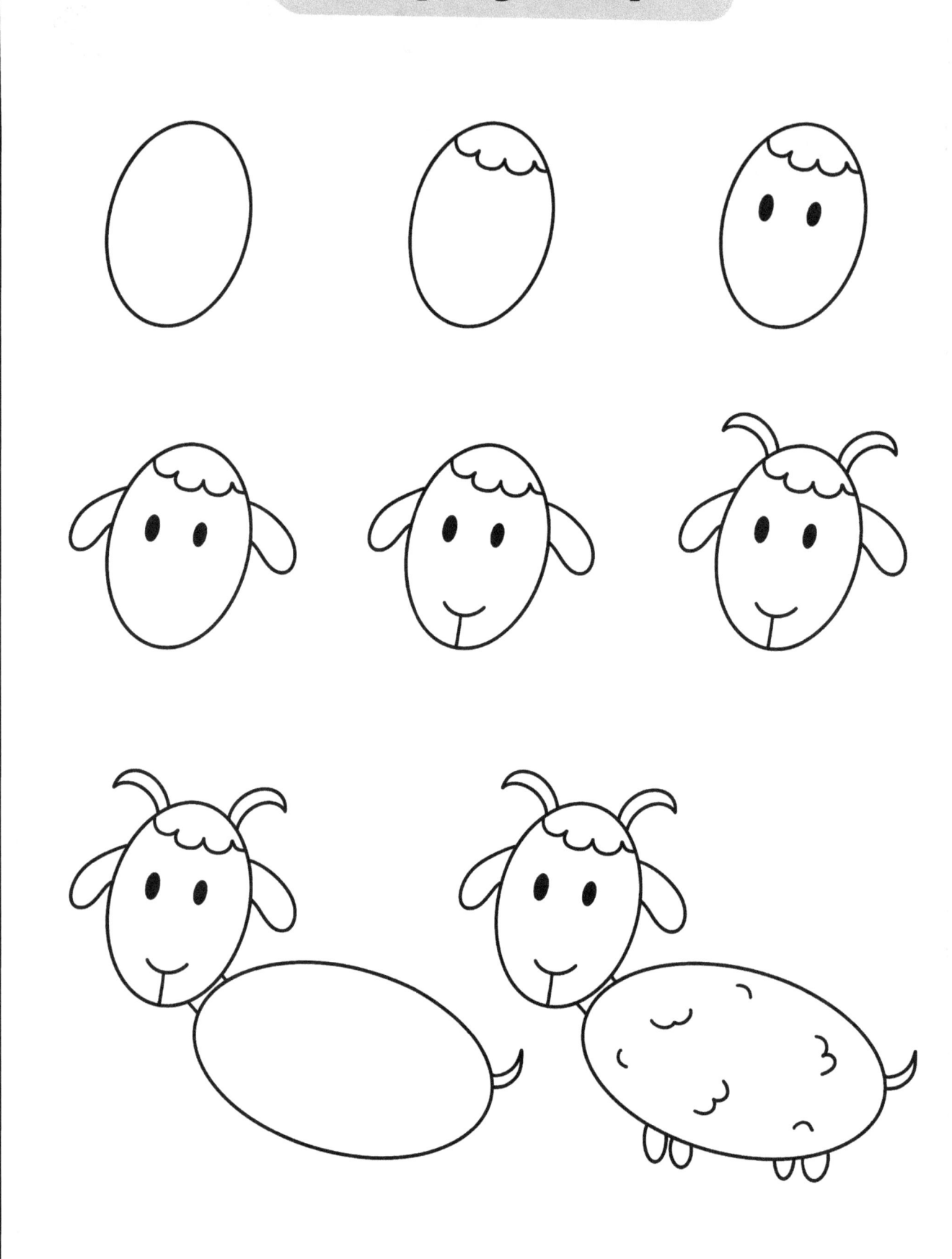

Step by Step

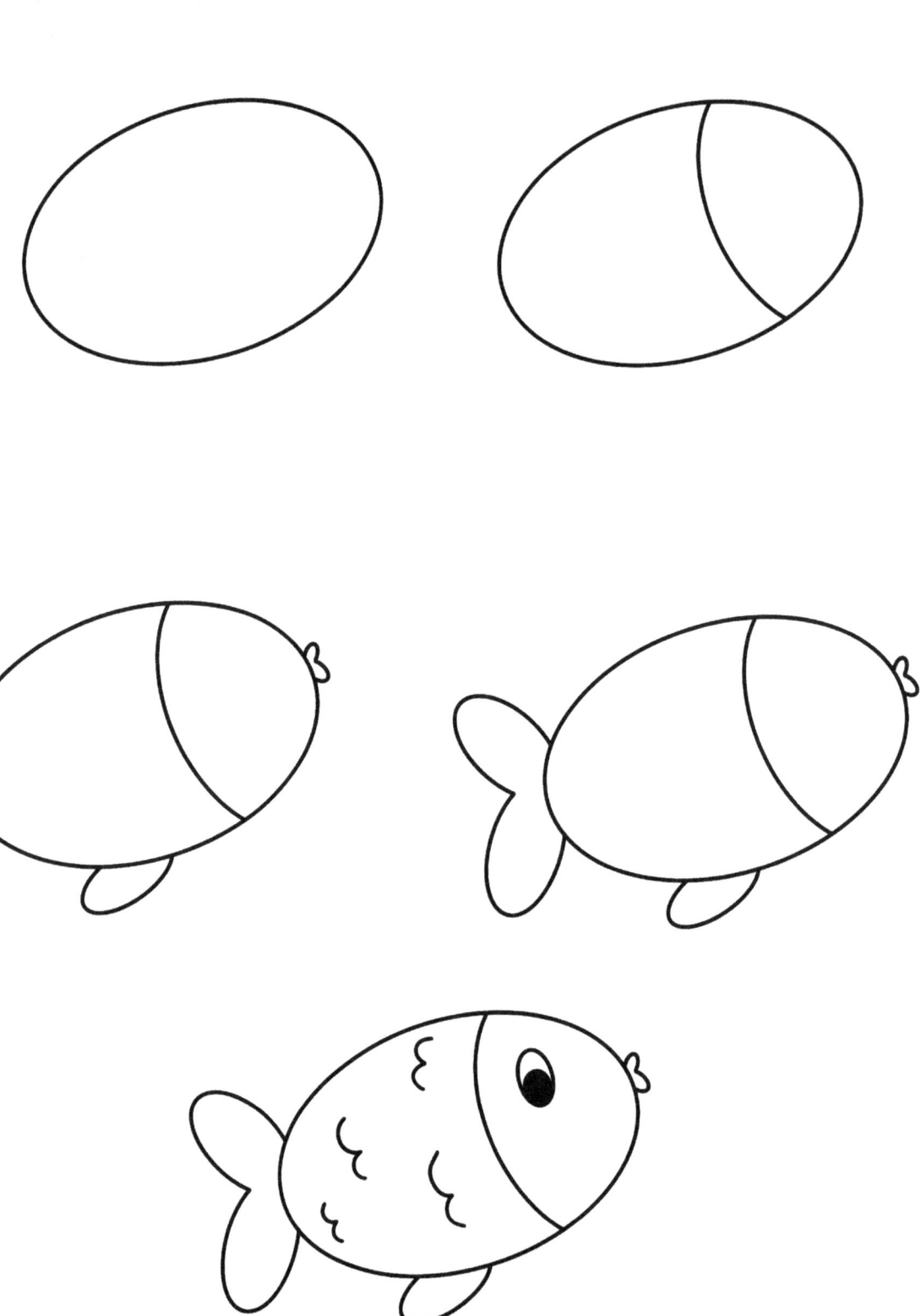

Step by Step

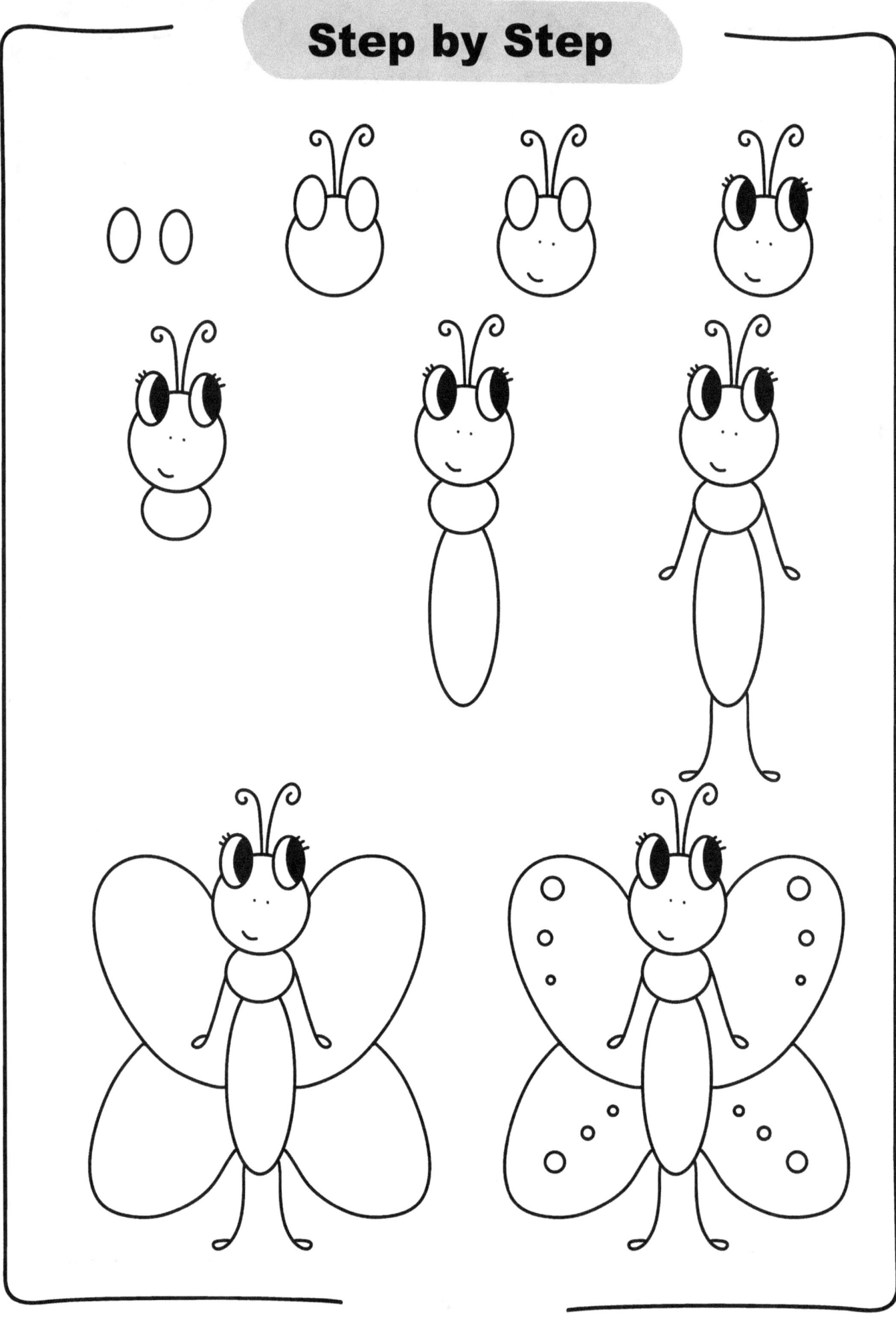

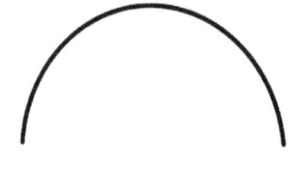
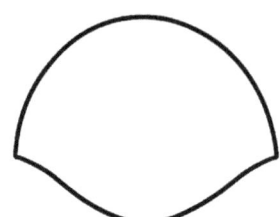
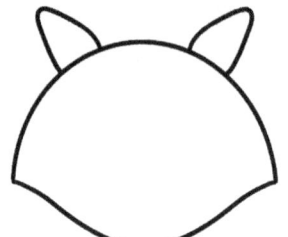
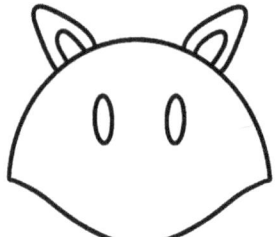
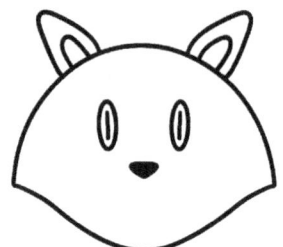
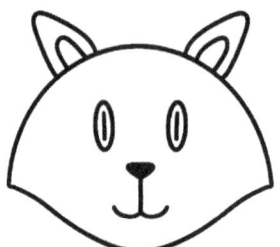
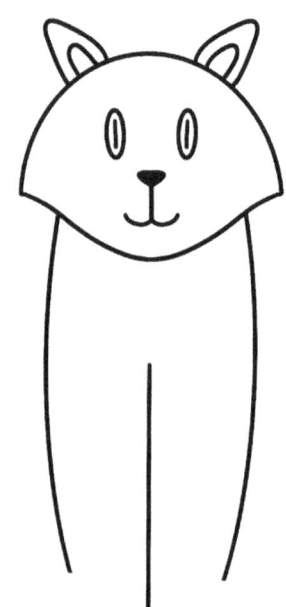
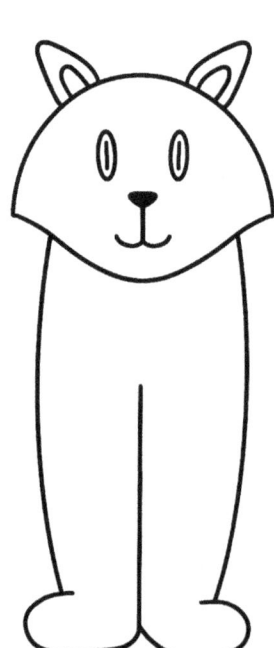
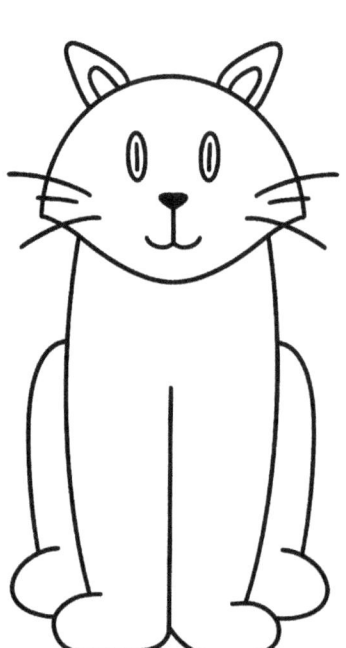

Step by Step

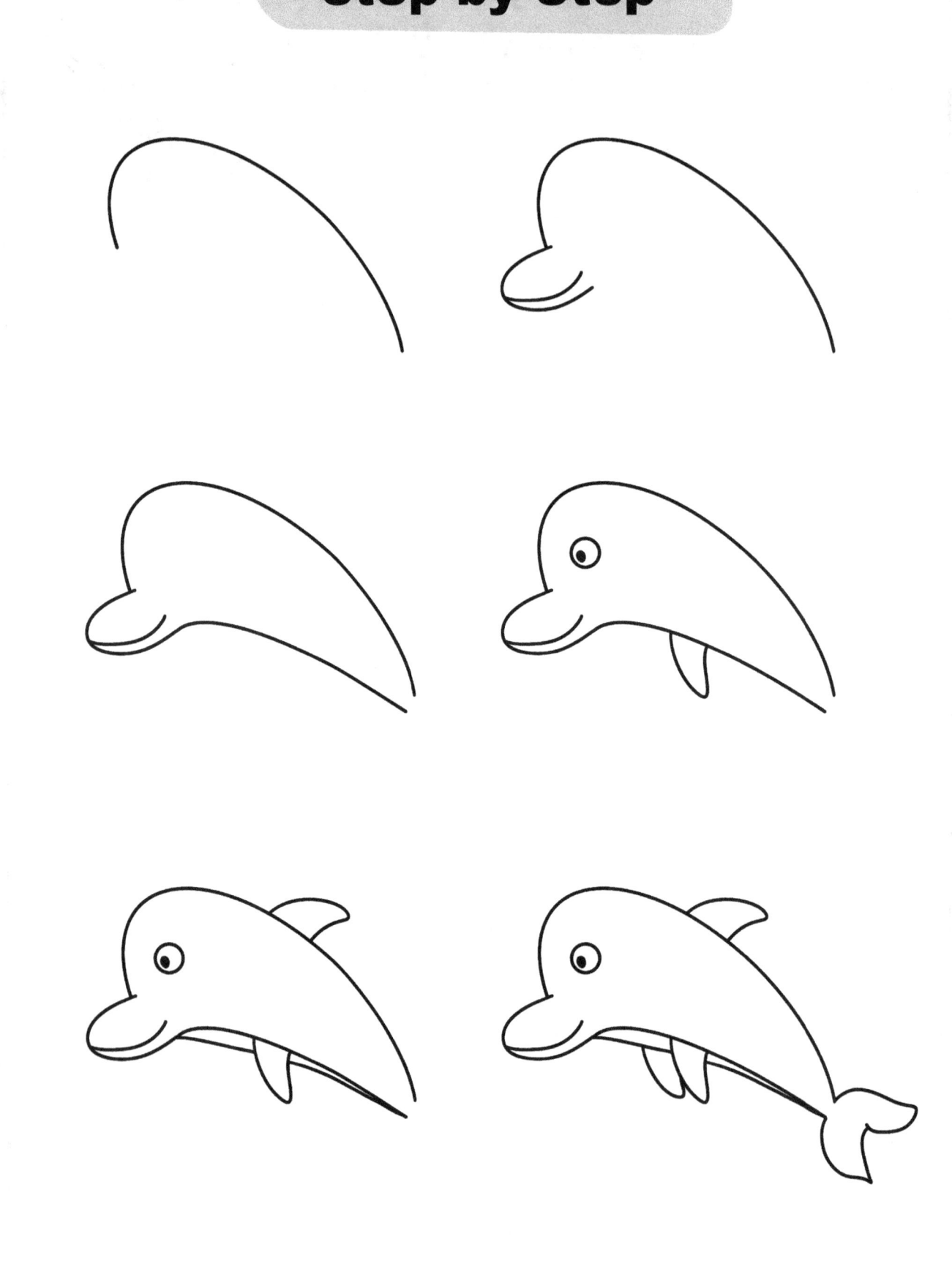

Step by Step

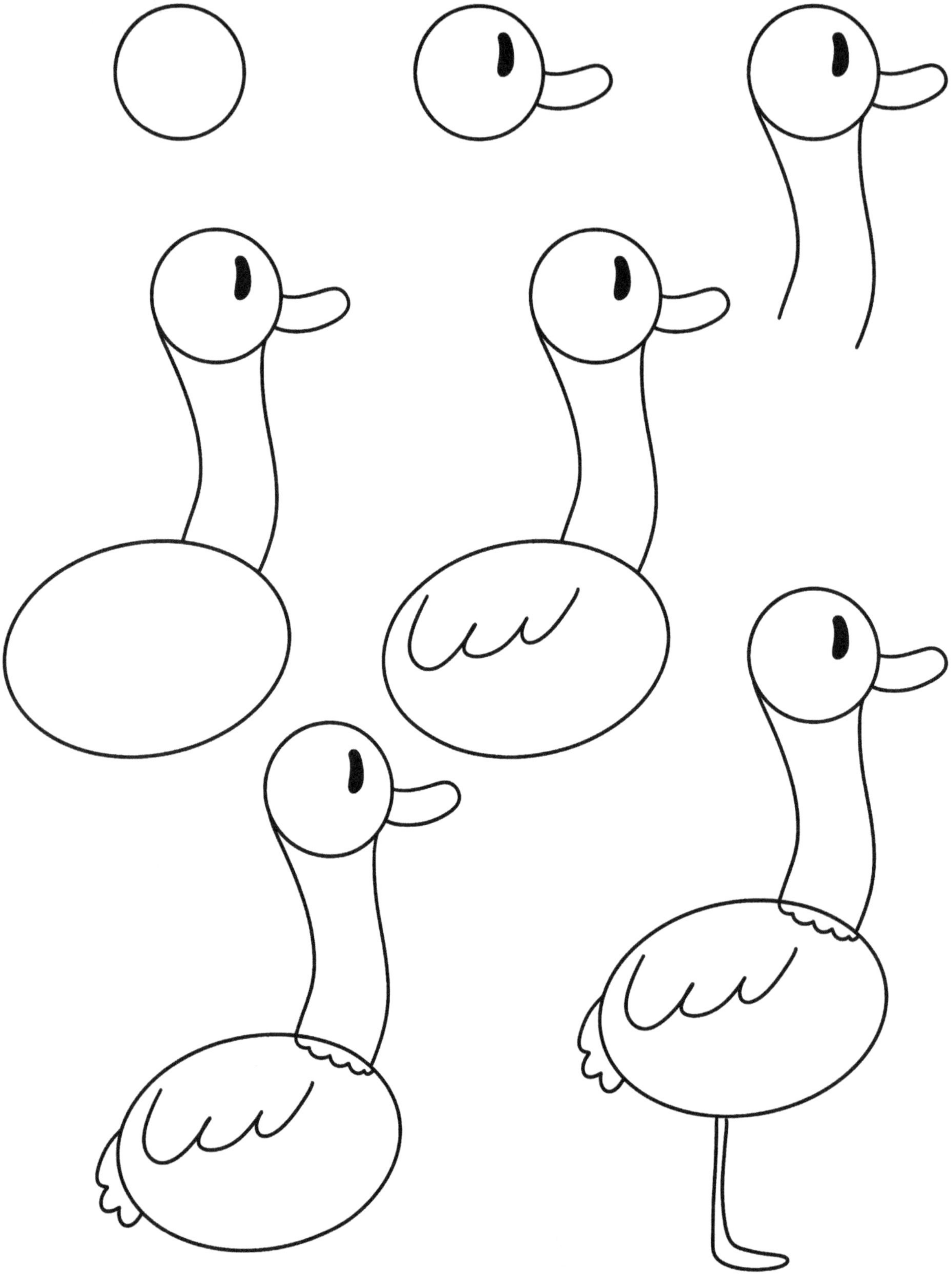

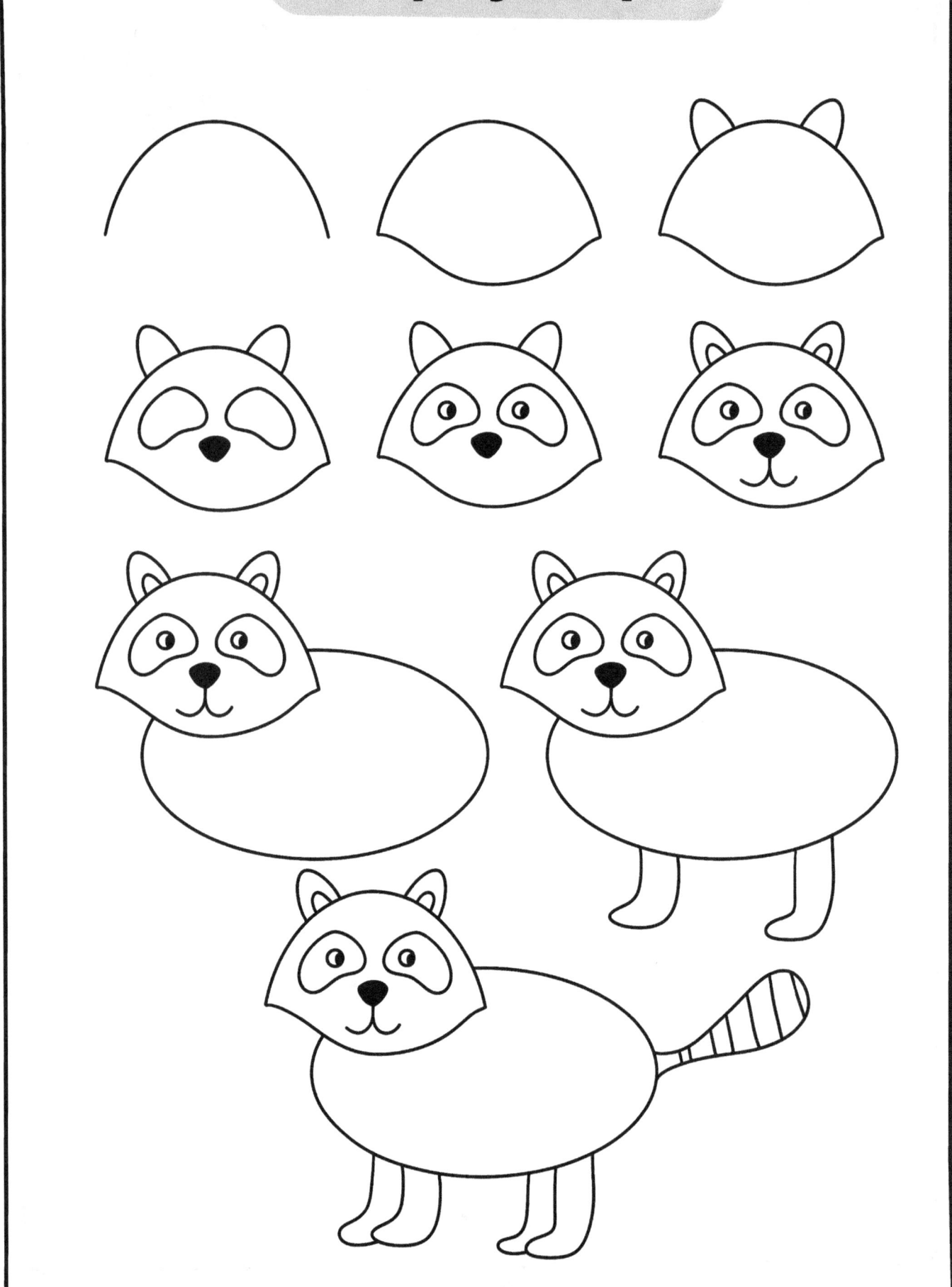

Step by Step

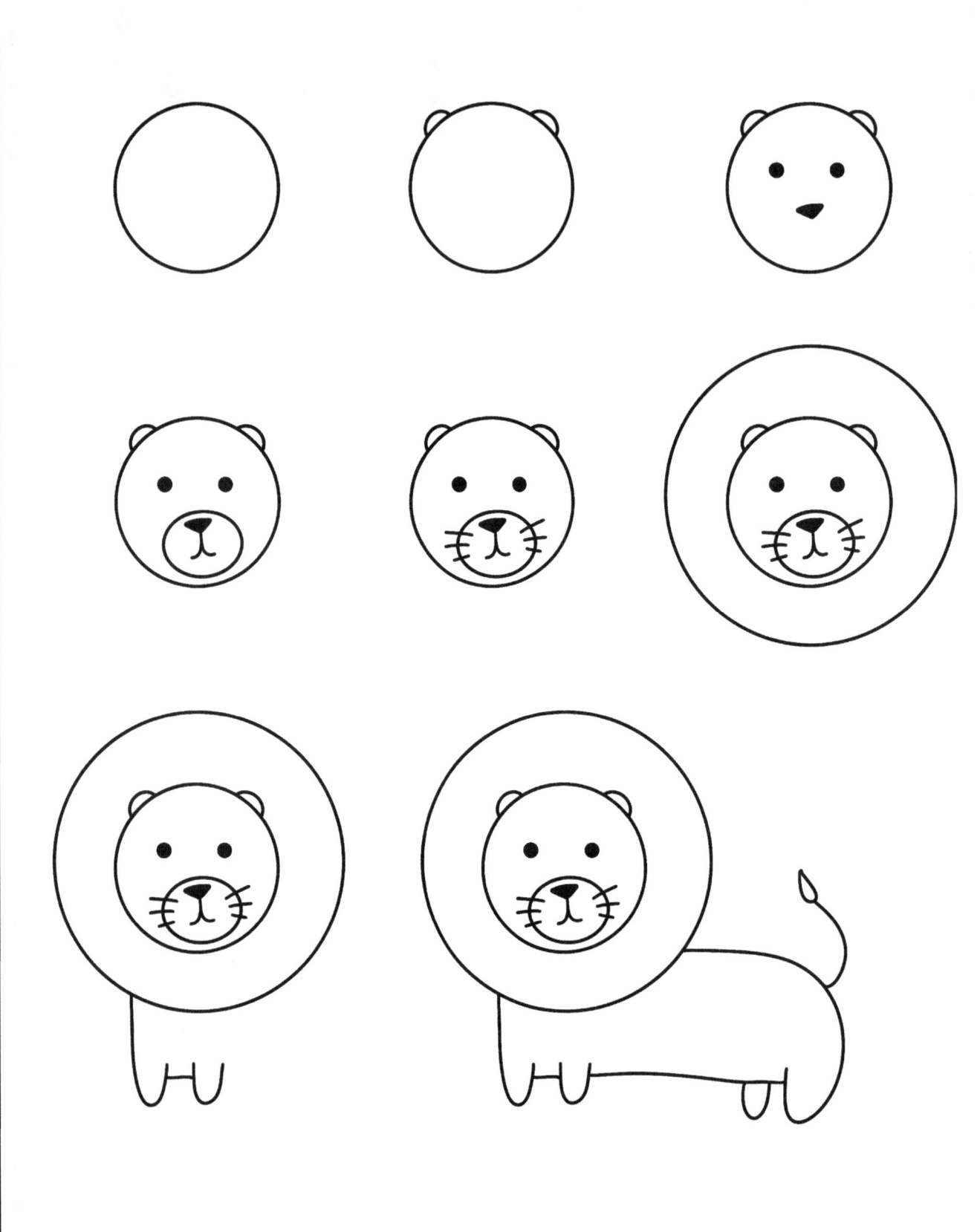

Step by Step

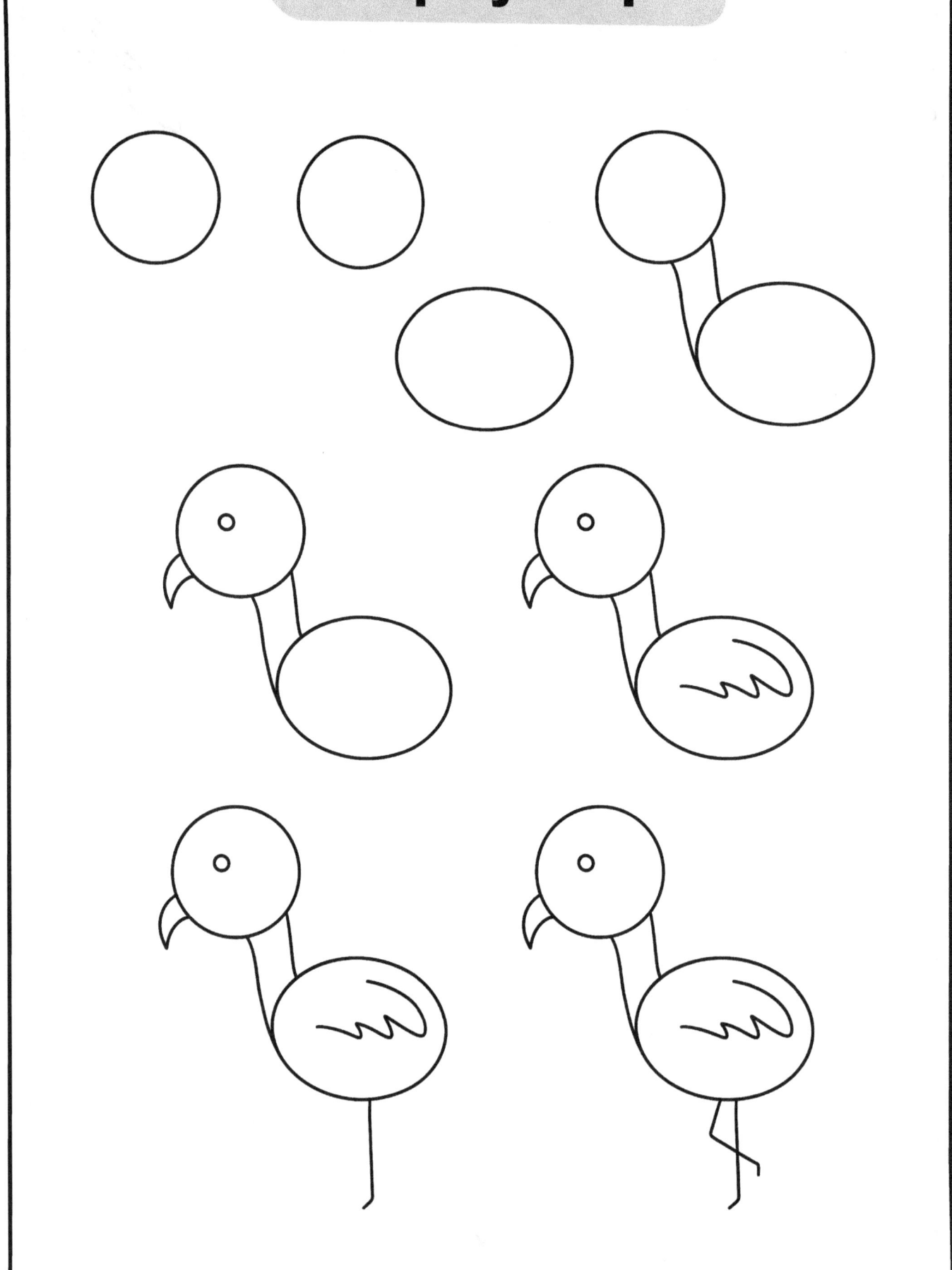

Step by Step

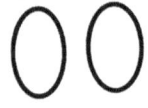 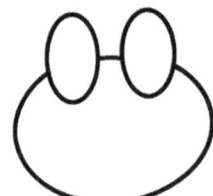 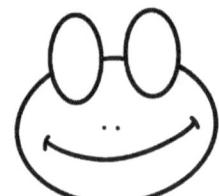

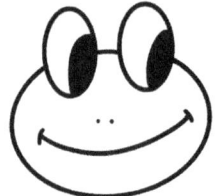 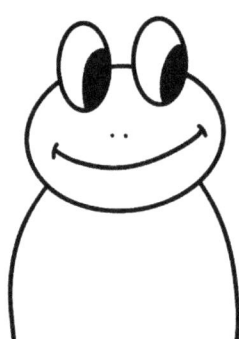 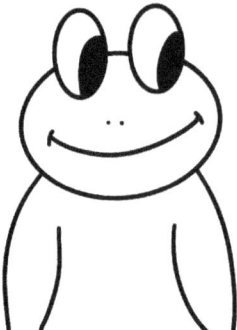

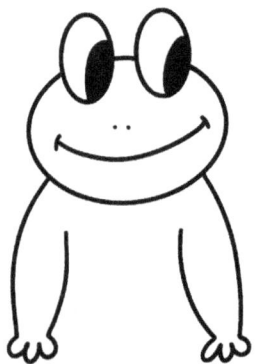 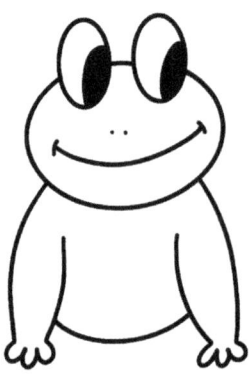 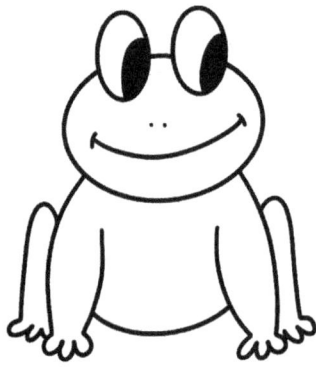

Step by Step

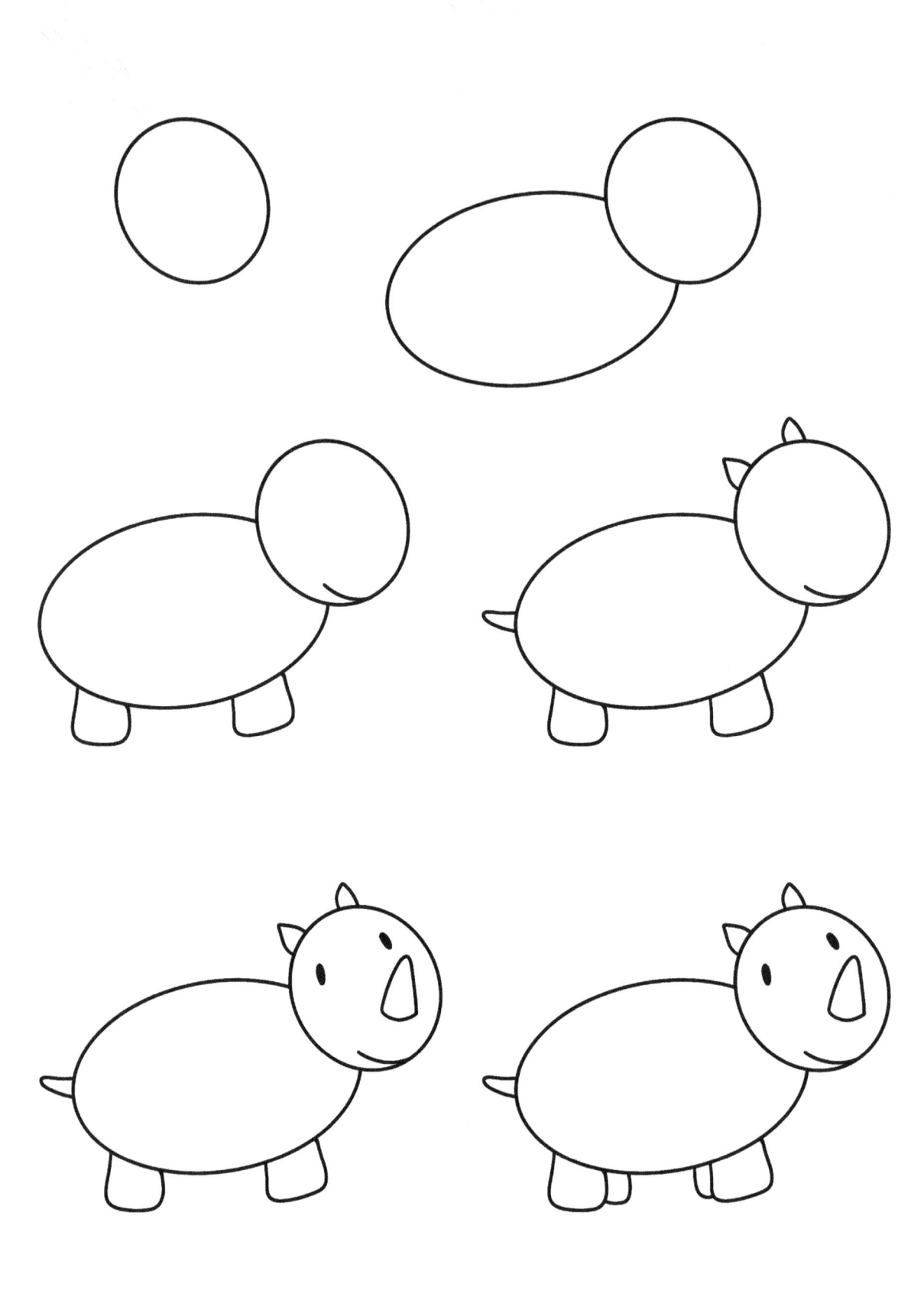

Share your artwork with community
and
get your FREE digital version!

Please kindly share it with us in the community.
Thank you so much. Visit our community here:

https://bit.ly/3BnaVgx

www.ingramcontent.com/pod-product-compliance
Lightning Source LLC
Chambersburg PA
CBHW080845220526
45467CB00008B/2392